BY ROBERT KELLY

Armed Descent (1961)
Her Body Against Time (1963)
Round Dances (1964)
Enstasy (1964)
Lunes (1964)
Lectiones (1965)
Words in Service (1965)
Weeks (1966)
The Scorpions (1967)
Song XXIV (1967)
Devotions (1967)
Twenty Poems (1967)
Axon Dendron Tree (1967)
Crooked Bridge Love Society (1967)
A Joining (1967)
Alpha (1968)
Finding the Measure (1968)
Sonnets (1968)
Statement (1968)
Songs I-XXX (1968)
The Common Shore (1969)
A California Journal (1969)
Kali Yuga (1970)
Cities (1971)
In Time (1971)
Flesh Dream Book (1971)
Ralegh (1972)
The Pastorals (1972)

Reading Her Notes (1972)
The Tears of Edmund Burke (1973)
The Mill of Particulars (1973)
A Line of Sight (1974)
The Loom (1975)
Sixteen Odes (1976)
The Lady Of (1977)
The Convections (1978)
Wheres (1978)
The Book of Persephone (1978)
The Cruise of the Pnyx (1979)
Kill the Messenger Who Brings Bad News (1979)
Sentence (1980)
Spiritual Exercises (1981)
The Alchemist to Mercury (1981)
Mulberry Women (1982)
Under Words (1983)
Thor's Thrush (1984)
A Transparent Tree (1985)
The Scorpions (new edition, 1985)
Not This Island Music (1987)

Editor

A Controversy of Poets (1965)

ROBERT KELLY

NOT THIS ISLAND MUSIC

BLACK SPARROW PRESS
SANTA ROSA ~ 1987

ACKNOWLEDGEMENTS

The poems in this book were composed between June of 1982 and September of 1985. They constitute the work I wish to present now from that time, apart from the long poem *The Flowers of Unceasing Coincidence* which will eventually be published separately.

Most of these poems appear here for the first time. A few were published first in *Conjunctions* (ed. Bradford Morrow), *Credences* (ed. Robert Bertholf), and *Threshold* (Belfast, ed. Dan Casey).

A small grant from the Faculty Research Committee of Bard College helped the preparation of this text for publication.

The poems called "Burnt Offerings," "The White Wall," and "The Rainmakers" were written in response to a remarkable series of lectures given by Robert Duncan at Bard College during 1982–83, and are dedicated to him.

LIBRARY OF CONGRESS CATALOGING-IN-PUBLICATION DATA

Kelly, Robert, 1935–
  Not this island music.

  I. Title.
PS3521.E4322N6   1987   811'.54   87-5181
ISBN 0-87685-693-8
ISBN 0-87685-692-X (pbk.)
ISBN 0-87685-694-6 (lim. ed.)

TABLE OF CONTENTS

TO THE READER (1)

My dear, my favorite person, for you all my life is work and all my work is play and you can read me or look away. Such power you have, to command me so, and such beauty, that to you I would over and over pour out everything I think, everything I can hear, everything I hear the words whisper, every sound I can steal. Truly you are my mother, for who else could I talk to in such confidence of being well heard? All the beauty I know is what I find in you, or let you find. You are my father and my lover and my child, and I am nothing without you.

Was it Colonel Fawcett's Expedition
in search of the lost Brazilian
city he called "Z" the old
characters called Ma-Noa
that came to grief, naked misery and leprosy,
as reported in the New York Journal American
early in the 1940s I find
this morning in the Enquirer as
found again, his long-limbed white
women still young, the colonel
wiser in all ways, alive as moss?

NOT THIS ISLAND MUSIC

VAMPIRE

for Bruce McClelland

What time do I have who have no time
for the old world the Borobodur
      the muse who by my ear
plucks me from pronouns to music
and I am gone (Stéphane,
      even as your matelot)
into another language of permissions
the discipline of listening is a lady too
      whose châteaux
are common as the moon on winter nights.

2.

And the sight of what symbol out of silver
induces what incisive trance
      in the lust-lathered beholder as
suddenly through winter casements
      chance-medleyed by the wind
half flown half stepping over the sill
      (sacred precincts of a house invading
invited by the space itself)
      he enters ravening
not in the form of bat or wolf but
      this same moon?

3.

No trick — a crucifix with moonlight on it
      silvering it. He stops
amazed at how his own light frightens him.
Since he is desire he is greed and since greedy
      needs every doctrine,
credits every catechism. The gods
are entertaining: they work a room

such as some great king or novel writer made
        interesting by sleeping one night in—
you read the bronze plaque on the wall
        and find the simple space made meaningful.

4.

So he stands arrested in his quest
for that other god, her flesh. Since he is greedy
        he is divided, dangerous.
Outside a russian wind strolls drunk through spruces,
        humid very, he sweats
to have knowledge of her. But this cross. Or crossed
        double dorje, or Vishnu's footprint.
Surely this patch of light on the carpet or yet
        still overhead and scummed with haze
the ground plan of the moon, itself a mandala.
How can he make his move among these sacraments?

5.

So language is in permanent détente
        always with gleaming fangs
scared of its proper meat. The virgin neck of things
        persists to lure me. That
is my Europe and my Orient. We have no past
        but what we want to do.
And I listen in my lusts for that uncharmed one,
sweet Nobody who does not cling. Even a gull
sometimes lets the fishguts drop, and flies away.
Black wing, white wing. I make my prey
        into a word I can speak.

16

MARRIAGE CONSIDERED AS AN ARRANGEMENT
OF OBJECTS IN SPACE

Going where for a wedding
to a door.
Buying a door, you start
with a hole
sensed in light,
a hole in a field
that shapes the field,
even standing there
without moving
you go in.

*

Start with a door.
Stand this up
at first aslant
leaning the lintel
on a star
and the blade on turf
till the door
listening
hears the whole earth.
When it hears
it stands.
Frame it in then
inside its jambs.

*

And the house
that random congeries
of the trivia of ecstasy
sorts itself out
behind the door,
is just there

suddenly
and you open it,
both,
you carry
your shadow
across the doorsill

some part of the shade
lingers on the threshold
to remind,
to show you
where the world went

and where Out is,
still green as ever,

the field.

*

Inside,
the honor of things
speaks its epic slowly.

Epic, because many,
because beginning
always in the middle of things,

because battle
when war comes
has dignity, beauty even,
and the peace
is more than truce,

epic
because life always wins,
because
it begins with *Who?*
and answers You.

*

Foot by foot
you learn the way.

And the floor you walk
is star-map

until the way
is everything you do.

Then at last
the house
gets up and moves.

Where, and why,
and how the curtain
hangs on the light

as if it and you
were parts
of one same thing.
And breakfast sings.

BURNT OFFERINGS

1. *The Fire Sacrifice*

I have stood at the right hand of the sacrificer
stirring red cloth tatters into rice
red beans barley spelt
sweet drops, the colors, till
mixed with cooking oil
it turned to fire in the fire.
He chanted
                    hurrying
things
        from this condition to that,
a wonder.
                    Song is all sending.

Ite, missa est. Our west
burns red for him, and Amitabha's garden
opens in the setting sun,
                            the celebrant
stirs until the transposition's done,
and this thought becomes that star.

And this lewd idea
vexing me halfway between
my hips and your lap

becomes a howler-monkey in Honduras green
waking a mother at false dawn
to check the damp forehead
of her sickly baby,
                        see,
the fever's broken, the child will live.

The *here* is what an animal cries,
and the here, heard, preserves the there.

2. The Letter

Unmistakable hand of an old man
the letter-forms still nobly spaced
but spidery, shuddery, window-struck,
gapped with new vistas.
Where the bookstaves, say,
don't close their loops
(an *o*, a *p*) or a greek *e*
trembles like a lover's lips
reading Dante to his sweet sophomore.

We read the text, a letter, say,
and say This man is old,
cold wasps hide in the woodwork of his heart
in serious doubt of springtime.
However brief his life now
he has been long.
                  Something buzzes.
How sweet the blood is still
(what *does* he still remember?
the girls? gulls over the Isle of Wight?
morning mist in a coombe up Overlook?
the taste of cheddar
cut for his mother
by the grocer when he was three
and the great orange wheel of it
rested on the barrelhead —

so much food, he loved
the taste of it, how could all
that food ever be eaten up
and only a few grains of day-rice left?

Yet it is all eaten now.
Yet it is still left,
the shiver and the lust in it.

We read the tremor in his alphabet.
His words like butter in butter-lamps

or Judaean yearlings that have been sacrificed.
What is here has been sent there.
When he wakes,
the crickets in his house
will all be silent,
he'll think he's young again.

And someone is.
Across the palimpsest
a soft-lipped reader waits,
tasting the losses of *this* life
into his young mouth—

a stinging, stirring medicine.
Homeopathic, we taste
each other in the mildest ways,
a little taste that was a man.

Haunted by the old man's life
the young man clarifies his own.
Every word is a letter from the dead.
>   *I lived my life for you*
>   *—but then we all do.*
There is nothing but this giving,
this sacrifice.

3. *The Recollection*

I must do it for myself,
this waking.
When all that is not myself
stands at my side
and stirs the wheat of sacrifice for me
and hands me the brassy yellow ladle
and churns in its own mouth
the butter I have to pour
untasted into fire.

This only fire
of the nascent day

my only song
is waking to

this long consenting to address
a voice from emptiness.

Cold street
you shiver on
I slip my jacket over
your thin shoulders
till the streetcar comes
up from the Embarcadero.
We're both cold, both
warm aboard, between,
you sit I stand
and then we sit together
uphill to my borrowed house
up the stairs
and past the light
and we are arms again
and what they hold,
shoulders and simple things,
limbs and laps in
nervous syntax being close.
You never knew how scared I was too —

and that the fear we so much shared
was the mutual oil we poured.

4. *The Stand*

Then who offers
and who burns
is not the question.
In the ardor of release
we read in the old man's
permissive penmanship
the old cosmology's revealed
that set the stars
so hard to read
— flecks of fat in the liver of the sky?

scattered barnyard of the light?
birds of omen stilled in flight?
as liturgy above his text.

I loved (he writes)
and this love of ours
like any blaze
was dangerous.
And while it feeds upon itself it lives.

24

Oh the Grail was a glad hotel
on a brave coast in a good time
and all the work we thought was world
was our vacation from

this real task: questless striving
to be the vessel into which pours
a serviceable radiance
the rest can drink.

To find the part of him that's woman
is a hero's prowess's final deed—
Achilles silk-hipped learns to weave,
or great-bowed Arjuna with kohled eyes

teaches meek-footed dance steps in the harem.

A SONNET FOR TED BERRIGAN'S *SONNETS* REPRINTED, INSTEAD ALAS OF THE REVIEW I PROMISED

It must be the whole world dont you think,
books on the edge of the table,
window, and across the street brownstone houses
like more books waiting to be read.
Eat everything on the plate, wash the dishes
spread out the ratty tarot cards and listen.
Further down in you than the tortellini fell
a congress of deceptions practices truth.
Listen, if we sat here after a big dinner
watching the sun fall into Jersey for a thousand years
it would never stop talking down in there.
And that's just the beginning isnt it,
since even these words we finally gasp out
are just scraps of a word you can almost remember.

MOMENT OF APHASIA

Find the word. If the found word doesn't come quickly, the sentence it purposed ceases to exist. The writer pauses, thinks, watches the grosbeaks squabble for seed in the courtyard, loses the drift of his thoughts, forgets the sense he thought he was making. He forgets the sentence. Then suddenly he sees the gaping syntactic wound where the fragment breaks off, and he runs to heal it with something plausible, not the sentence but a sentence, any sentence, to flee the horror of an incomplete proposition. He writes it down and hurries on.

From all such hastily improvised statements, no one of them intended, the world may well have been made.

THE WHITE WALL

"A white wall is the paper of a foole."
George Herbert, *Outlandish Proverbs,* #839

Stare at the wall.
Say what you see.

And what you say
leaves no trace,

no famous poem, no earned dollar, thaler,
to make you infamous. You are a fool

to listen to me.
A piece of white

paper is a foole's
wall
     and only it

to set between him and the north wind,
the scouring santanas of economic adversity,

a crumbling wall
he cant even stand on
to look good
in the eyes of the girls of the town.

"The wild child slept by the oiled shoe"
he smiled in his sleep and if he smiled
the standers-by judged him a fool —
    'He goes to school
    to a sheet of blank paper,

    studies a white wall
    and smiles without a sense of humor,

                smiles without wit.'

Shy an apple at the moon,
you silly little,
                    and put the light out
that shows us the paths in our conventional minds

(an apple lodged in the moon's face
decaying there,
crater in the stone, a drinking bowl, brave)

the fool sees just a birdbath in the sky.

Follow the fool
on his eastern journey
gone to meet Capella
rising but meets Algol there,
engages scarlet evil
for the sake of trust.

'See where he sleeps in his shoes,
could his mind be travelling, contending?'

'He has no mind, he cannot talk,
what happens in his head is weather only,
thunderstorm and breezes, bricks without mortar'

'But maybe he listens as he sleeps,
he has ears at least, one pressed
to the earth and one turned up to us'

'Makes no more sense than a puddle of rain,
no more sense than a whistle, than a copper penny
lost in the mud when bread is dear'

Any stone can tell a fool
what the wise men of the town
find hard to voice
though they too at midnight
coming from the House of Prayer
catch a glimpse of it and

a word that might survey it
rises but not reaches their lips
— yet it takes the whole
sky full of stars to tell them
what a cobblestone says to the fool.

Inside the stone there is a well
where nothing fell.

Pure, the water always rises
from a beginning
below all our feet.

From it the fool drinks copious assent,
says yes and yes and yes again
and always yes. What is there
to refuse he finds?

* * * * *

"over the gritty conversations and back,
round designs without lines"
expanding like a vague but comforting idea
(likely I will not die today,
there's some cheese in the icebox, funds
in the bank, a girl I know is fond of me)

we feel a fine moon rise mumbling in the trees.
Somehow this light will make us better —
and it will have no effect on the fool.

A fool is all effect and nothing happens.
He is a pure result of which the whole world is the cause.

'Is he the stone'
he looks in?'

'He is what floats
and makes it swim.'

'In our river?'

'There is no other.
Here is a map of it
running from the wheatfield to the ear
of the mayor's pink daughter.
None of the boys in the town
have swum so far yet,
and no one knows if she can hear it.
She will not listen, and her mother says
"You do not listen." '

                    The fool listens.
His sleep is heroic, sheer hearing
void of answering.

(Assent is no answer. Assent is the first
      question and the last.)

He hears the windows of the town,
delicate gamelan effects of shimmering moonlight
chilling tiny tremors in the glass he hears.

Envoi

Count the words the fool doesnt say
and say them to my love for me,
silent sideways poem.

If I were wise I would be silent too,
but when I look on her
I grow foolish with listening.

Bring her my trouble and keep
acknowledging some things are permanent.
She is, I am, we are, and hearing is.

THE RAINMAKERS

for Robert Duncan

The groups of God
broken into world,
morsels chosen
from that curious Hellenistic author
The Demiurge
whose multitudinous works
we daily anthologize,

persuaded by French masters
and local mistresses
to be wise,
                    to live in a world
(this one)
if only for the sake of the weather.

They run the weather,
the rainmakers
want us to like it,
sell us the sexy
isotherms of semiotics,
the structure of structure,
                    o Fashion
is a savage god.

        2.

Poetry tries "to bring all its experience into natural grace"
says Duncan, and keeps the numbers
current,
        the swells of speech
whose ordered passion
compels the restless lust of mind
into the presiding metaphor of dance
which here knows itself
as particulate movements

32

studied in noticeful economy,
physicist at cloud chamber
charming the incidents
to hold some place in natural speech
(trying to be natural!)
as if it really were a world we speak.

3.

And the numbers are not governors,
the numbers are white, every one is one,

wings of a jungle bird
analyzed into color as
one thing listening always to another,

an old woman visiting her bees.

POUSSIN

As an exacting inference of a small other century crawling around on its knees along the Aubusson looking for a small lost diamond, Poussin pleases. The grammaticality of his pictures, much admired, is the polite palaver of a man with something else on his mind. The alert eye is that of someone who has lost a small and precious thing—but one that could be easily forgotten, even lived without in a sleepy lackluster way of life—and who now attends to every item in the visual field—the pattern, even the weave, of the carpet, say—to be certain it doesn't conceal the object of his search. The thing isn't there, of course, and the scrutiny of what *is* there becomes paranoid in its intensity (lest he forget!), reaches as paranoia always does backward for master-plans, conspiracies, a theory behind all theories. But it isn't there either. Whatever was on his mind is not in his paintings. But his mind is.

When I was twenty I was sure
I could rule a kingdom if they needed one.
At forty I began to notice
there were days I forgot to water the aloes
and dust settled on the television screen.

Now I wonder if even these words
have as much authority as I think, as the ink
a true man writes his letter with
to a girlfriend, or quick note to his
mother saying "My dearest
you are old, I dont want you to die,
how can I ever tell you my love
except by being as much as I can
the man you suffered to make me be?"

You cant write that way to your mother.
Not yet am I ready to occupy
the empty throne cushioned
in sun-faded damask silk.
The courtiers stand around waiting
with hands in their sleeves, sneering.
Sea-wind shifts brocade round their skinny ankles.

Bittersweet growing up the red wall
old factory empty at the foot of Waterman

and across the Seekonk
the houses and wharves and bait shacks of East Providence
these
          are poignant, these are art.

and if the Parthenon crumbles under our carbon monoxide
we can build it again
                    by formula,
          Christ, we could carve it out of soap,
                                        but these
                    are the actual
                    colors
                    the structures
                              of living,
                                        this is tantra
the continuity
              of actual effort
                              no two buildings alike
                    and in the quarry of time
cut out to be different by men
              wanting at most to be agreeable and cheap
and they stand in their difference and what will we do
when these are gone,
                    there is no rule that remembers them

                    these brittle facts
              hem of the absolute,
colors of old houses distinct as

the breasts of actual different women in their chlamyses
their shirts annotated by the wind
                              passing
by a shack on the hither shore selling menhaden and eels
among the skeletons of wild carrot and tansy.

                                        Providence

POETIC RAPTURE READS FACT TOO

It isnt all about sex and squirrels.
It perpends. It calculates a departure
into the heart of a woman or a star,

it understands science into life stages,
it teaches tango. Touch me,
immaculate Things, mandalay me

with your minstrel moons,
carpenter my easy doubt with seasoned oak.
I read your oracles in the triflingest.

ON BEING ASKED TO TAKE PART IN A PUBLIC READING OF WHITMAN'S *SONG OF MYSELF* 'FOR DIFFERENT VOICES.'

But I am not a different voice,
I am the same voice endlessly reviewing
options of earth
so I cannot pour from the pitcher like raw milk daffy with cream
or slop dazed in the churn on my way to coming.
I am no fish to the subtle purse-seines of eternity,
their silky webs grazing our secular shallows
where I do dart and do insist and do get loud
calming the fears of my gonads with ceaseless activity.
And I do number Beloved the hairs on your heads, the dense
tangles interwoven at the gates of your womb.
I am a pilgrim but I jog before no archaic Ka'aba,
I walk up and down the length of the day questing to devour
the sunny contours of accurate flesh, your bodies in motion Beloved,
the swing of your hips as you open a door and vanish
from my sight at the window though it is my own house you are
    entering,
come to join me at our Palestine below the counterpane.
I am all about time but not in time included,
my dactyls invoke a sybil who does not lust unbeing but
Emptiness, brightness of animal vacancy flourish a gone self,
self gone and that be the blazon to lead my troops of petitioners
gladly through the Eros of dictionaries, the marble terrazzo of banks,
the riverside spangled with secretaries, with pigeons, each one of
    them
vistas my city better than I can for all of my cunning.
Old Whitman who sang he was a self and was several until he was
    many,
no self he. But I confuting
declaring my selflessness stay noisily the same,
the smell of me rank on the poem
as ailanthus stamens over Brooklyn streets on June evenings
when the streetlamps come on and madden the coveys of bats
strafing the branches, warmth of puberty nights.

THE VIRGIN AND THE FIG

She stood before a limestone wall
and darkened whitewash with her shadow.
The sun ripened her the way it does
and down below the burden of the lawn

every body carries, a small scarlet liberty
was ripening too. We are fruits
to each other, and we grow for others
what feeds us only when we give away.

A virgin thought, a sad trombone
walking the Dakotas. A farm, a sorrow.
In the latitudes of her lap was growing
a tropic ecstasy the wind was tasting now,

had come there for it from the Pole
thousands and thousands of miles
as if on this whole continent only she
had something to nourish us poor creatures with.

BY THE AMERICAN SHORE

I want to find a house
I have never lived in
on a beach not frequently
visited. I want a wave

that never crested before,
I want a door
entered only by people
who dont understand me

and I dont understand.
The wallpaper should be green
and the fireplace burn coal.
The women on sofas cross

their legs at the angle and go
in summer to mountain relatives.
The men have little to say.
Give me a glass of water

from that clean sink and one
slice of tomato from the fridge
and turn down the Shaker quilt.
Then, then I will have lived.

Stamford

I snarled at the rose seller
"you call that a rose?"

yet it was red and had the smell
roses had when I was a little boy
as if a lady stood nearby
and I knew all that
but there was something I didnt know

and only now have news of,
disagreeable almost,
murmuring partridges in the underbrush
bringing me intelligence of love.

SWANS

So many swans here in Connecticut
on the shore, where the frozen canal
mouths the unfreezable sea,
swans with a lot on their minds:

What are people up to, what
are they really about? We try
to understand what is most difficult,
this love for a self not like the self.

Our own long practice is love mirrors,
calm shallows, sleek early ice,
monogamy of close resemblances—
we mate for life the animal we are.

But what do they see, whose eyes
meet no resemblance when they meet?
Why is there so much silence
in the cognitive domain?

Once they cherished us for our chaste
gaudiness, romantic love,
our fabulous fidelity, strength delicate
or just our rich brown meat.

Now we are only beautiful,
and that we fly is an embarrassment to them,
a rumor of impermanence, a hated
murmur about dead kings.

DIFFERENCE

The lift is ominous. There is a cable that beneath the streeted hill connects the falling car with a restraining wheel. This lets us down. And later, when we've reached the valley, at Columbus, say, its contradictory motion will draw us up Russian Hill, that faraway, that the quiver-fleshed blonde strippers at the Peppermint Tree dream about living on if only. If only the car went up by itself. If only the land had a king and the king had a son and the air was filled with bright birds, quetzals, say, whose freely let fall feathers could be gathered loosely and with ease from the ample shrubbery and sold for a small fortune at a market you know about. Then we would see what all that nakedness is about. Then beauty would be its own reward, and the prince who came to gawk would stay to court and woo and win and bring his brides (for he needs many) back with him up to his marble palace on the hill, where they could wear clothing whenever they chose, or not, and lie about in the leafy zenana or stand not exactly posed by the balustrade on the immense veranda beneath which the sea's amorous waves would keep up an endless tumult of applause. And after luscious months of such living they would say it's not so very different from what they knew. Love didn't make all the difference we thought it would. Nothing can ever be very different from what we know.

If I were a crescent moon
beneath the spillway of some reservoir

I'd set to glisten myriads
of silvery simulacra of me and in each

a knob of black sky would be clutched
or cradled or jiggled

by the uneasy waters trying
to settle down for the night.

When water's quiet there is only
one moon in it. This is me.

I look upon myself and fancy
untold orgasms in time to come—

the bright sickle that I am
will gleam above abrupt conventions

that spell out revolutions.
A new Robespierre will swear

his virgin oaths on me, on me
Saint-Just will rely for metaphors

of well-concealed lubricity
and a new Marat will turn

slow his noble head from side to side
without finding anyone at all to trust.

Again and again. I see myself
in the lost hopes of populations,

lost ideals of agitators, lost
dreams of drunkards cold sober at dawn.

Only the lip of me left in the sky
after my tender word is said and gone.

THE VENUS OF MOUNT RUTSEN

The snow-woman we've seen all week,
big-breasted, big-hipped, small
headed, is much melted now
by the side of Mount Rutsen Road.

It has come to her by day
and the warm diminishing
is registered each cold night
and held there one more day.

Today her breasts are gone
almost and her head's
a little prong. But the enormous
shapeless hips are where

the upper body's gone.
She is palaeolithic now, cave mother,
naked opportunist of pure womb

as if this road and this town too
were fecund, and spring would come
here fantastically and soon

and we would beat the world at mating,
the snow in sunshine glinting
like the eyes of young wives.

WHAT THE WAITRESS AT DUNKIN DONUTS SAID
TO ME

"Trouble me, trouble me   the plain white bread
working for a living   full of air this dough
a bread is air we eat   but that also is santana
parched wind howling down Rubio Canyon   that also
kamikaze   godwind   go crazy   "trouble me
trouble me I am bored out of my mind   behind
this counter   show me your heavy rocks   your burning
sand   sand discussion sand philosophy   the taste
give me something sweet for my coffee   can I trouble you
sweet and low   "trouble me   lead me
into the fire where the sand burns into glass   how bright
this single glass will be   diamond in my poor world
that will not glisten   "listen, trouble me
till I'm out of control   listen to me till my face
is scarred with your attention   it is terrible
to be all day long   "trouble me   it is not Eros
and not a rose   it is cloth under cloth
and every weave   oppresses my skin   with its mark
I am pressed   by my fancy   the sunlight even
is like sand in the air   you who have been California
the size   the size everything is   "let me come home
with you inside me   look at me   just sitting here
with the sand up to my knees   the heat of it only
sucking my heat   "trouble me   burn myself away
till no one is left   for them to trap   in the sandy hours
days that once seemed numerous   no broken   a piece
of clock is all that's mine   night to cool out and dawn
to dread   always back here   an art of suffer   and never
know the other sides of mountains   books promised me
"trouble me   against the hex of work   give me an image
inside me conscious   to that country   where every
moment has its moment   no touch without a mind to notice
no skin without its touch   no road without a sun on it
trouble me   let me go there   no leper without his fated kiss.

48

A CONTINUITY

The persistent manifestation of change
under the gloss of lustrous seeming permanence
is what the stream had to tell her. "I am a name
that lingers while the things I am run by."
So much was obvious. Run dry. Persistent
enactment of what isnt even there to mean
is what the telling told her, "I have told
myself a story in a million voices
and called it the world." Antiphons of anthracite,
bauxite transports, keels of old ships, trimarans.
No one walking down this street with me, and turning
south off gravel into the myrtly woods would

on coming to these cataracts and the swimming hole beneath
suppose a more durable romance than a fly
trapped on a window screen or, more prettily, some tiny
white violets crouched in the shadow of chianodoxas,

sky blue flowers, themselves quite small, here for a week then gone.

THE CRY OF I

[*after W. H. Hudson*]

Blas Escovar, who killed an ox by shouting at it,
raising his big bass voice, a gentle man but tried
severely by his ox over and over getting tangled
in its traces now has a dead ox in his furrow

and a doubt about how to live. We hurt people,
that is clear. Even by sympathy a magic
web is woven, out of love indeed, that meshes
our unwary lovers in a thin-drawn cry

—trailing y-glide of the diphthong of my name—
the I that wraps itself around the other and
that one sound brings them to the ground.
You are trapped in my sense of myself, my sense of you

is also a jungle. I can do nothing but notice this
and keep my voice down and murmur very softly
what I cant keep from speaking altogether
and hope for the best. As Blas Escovar thereafter

talked soft to his wife, his black farm hand, his little cat.

CANZONE

What is evident becomes a flower
"the clitoris of earth" he
called it, and she "a planet

is all spirit; we alone
contribute musculature to it,
the delicate erectile,

the thrill." One ruddy tulip,
two voices mingling like lips
like lips saying a word

and the word honest, full of seas,
that is. And he essayed again:
"How can it not love you,

this animal I am?" But she
was dancing then, even in morning,
even in rain, and it had, her dancing,

the same kind of indecency
the flower had, too red, too beautiful
to endure the scant mercies of the day

while beads of water
slipped into the tight-petalled chalice
or stood outrageously still on her lips.

SENSATION

Back in the old days
when the human american body still
(it must have been 1965)
had plausible sensations
a man stood in an empty room
in Boston. To whom
a woman entered
and they touched.
Touched a lot,
made out just standing there
and the sun came in the dusty windows
and winter traffic fumbled down Beacon Street
audibly an alley away.
They feared to lie on the dirty floor
or feared each other
too much to lie down.
And the fear turned into feeling
and the feeling worked.
But they—or so they—
never did it again,
never went (as they both
thought of it, quaintly) further.
And years (or but years) later,
in the middle of all the
everything else
each of them knew they had
come as far as there is to go.
This is you, and this is me
and here between us suddenly
an energy where we are not two.
And there is no between.
And then there was—
even their last caresses on the stairs
down to the street were closures,
formal, epilogue and undertow.
He thinks back: I knew

her body then, better than my own.
And she: things
seldom look like our names for them.
Love is easy. That was feeling.
Horncall. Deer vanishing over the hill.

YUCATAN

for Elizabeth Robinson

The pyramid at Kabah   which you can see   only if   you are attentive
and climb   by the act of 'dense matted jungle'   nakedly walking
across the field   is it a field   naked watching   *does*
anything grow there   if   does   this pyramid no one   has ever
opened   did you   beyond the milpas   squatting like them
becoming an extrusion of the natural simplicity of time   the earth
is not something to be noticed   they stood   did you stand
and was the   sky different the stars   inside your old house
in your own skin   lights   dear life   the corn goddess shits corn
and between what grows and what was never   walk attentive   if you
said if you said if   and only   would the hill become a hill
that otherwise was the same flat earth   all that way to find horizon
you who were born of no mother   born in the arms of a man   dark
himself standing up on rock   to hold you   up to the sky and keep you
from the sky   from any remembering   before you ate corn   the mud
dries in the middle of winter and   in brackets we see   in
brackets we love   or are forgotten   your father's arms containing
like horizons your soft discomfort   when any woman has stood   upon
an artificial mound erect   near sea or lake or forest   she
in new relation with   the powers   the powers   she must reach
out to any fire that she finds   however it may burn her   if she is
attentive   this sensation to climb   a different hill   becoming.

54

RECESSIONAL

Spyan ras gzigs la na mo

Into the underneath—

the used teabag
is drying among ashes,
stained delicate mauve—
hibiscus flowers in it
and the gamboge of chamomile.
Meanwhile she reads Proust.

The places lust conducts me to,
a cup, a fallen petal
from a ruined anemone,
sly fiftiesish jazz ooping along
in or as grey daylight.
How much meat there is on the bone!

Not much in this culture
left for me. I will arise
and go into the future,
to the country I take it
joggers are also trotting to
beyond quiche and croissants,
beyond the poignant resurrections
each commodity promises and fails.

I see a rough grey gravel hill there
I am suddenly determined to climb
and set a pebble down to praise
all those who came before me
knowing no more than I do of the way.

PERSONAL HISTORY

I am a dethroned descendant of kings, too poor to repair my forefathers' palace you see in ruins all round me. There is no reason any longer to withhold this information from you. Already you must have guessed, if only from the paltriness of my gifts. When it comes down to it, I have nothing to give but myself, and I have given that away so many times there's hardly any courage in the gift. How many times can one give oneself away—a good question, this, to ask a woman. I ask it, if only to explain the nervous silence with which I welcome any assent. To what can I welcome you? Come with me, I say, but the coming is only me and only you, and where are we then when we have come, say, come and gone and come again and where are we?

On a clear day you can see, faintly, the lines of the old walls. This ash tree, itself moribund, once stood in a paved courtyard, the Court of Ill Dreams, and was soothed by water dribbling from a naiad's silver lips into a silver basin. Now it casts its spell on grass and rubble, rubble so finely divided and ground up it looks like ordinary dirt and gravel. This was a house, and I its lord by rights am hardly more than a man standing up at evening, casting a big shadow but being no bigger than I am. How big is that?

To the old king a druid came one day and spelled: Your children will be intricate and few; the line they inaugurate will be of poor men, eloquent and bold and self-defeating, comely till old age and never to be relied on. Rightly guessing Beauty to be the cheapest of Nature's tricks, they will be beautiful and cultivate beauty and talk from dawn to dawn in words that will last longer than they will—and right they should, the words the best part of them by far. They will put all their strength and cunning into this cheap palavering.

The old majesty my once father asked: Why this? And the druid answered, Such is the way with men and things, why should this house be an exception? And my once father was silent, bowed his head and went to beget me on his wife the queen.

56

As far as you can see when you stand beside me, just so far are the limits, *temenos,* of my ancient palace. Right here you stand with me in the old bedroom, the *thalamos* of the kings, and where the old wood floor creaks below our feet the tile tesserae glittered once, and the bed that made my blood spread vermilion and gold in the center.

When I survey you, smooth line of your hip, fastidious upwelling of your breasts, I suppose myself enthroned again, lord of some promise, such that I can reach out my hand and bear some meaningful relation to the world I see. Not mastery but use. Not ownership but awe. When the descendants of kings are poor, they have no hope but what they speak and what they touch. Monarch of my skin and of my speech, no more than that. And I have my own fastidiousness, a conscience even as the clergy say, not to bring you boldly to a room with no floor, a wall with no door, a bed with no bottom, a dream with no waking — the place I live now. And yet I touch you.

LE POÈTE DE 14 ANS

I was trying to be beautiful with lousy tools,
fried food and crowded avenues, a botanical
garden of tight dresses on jampacked buses.
So I got to be shabbily beautiful and that's
not nothing. I walked around a lot
stupefied by everything I saw,
never really sure how much I wanted
what I wanted so much, or how much I wanted
to get into a yellow european car and drive
out to the end of the road and listen
to the droll boredoms of natural order
tree after tree. Wood does a lot of complaining.
When you watch a brook shushing over rocks
the first thing it washes away is your life,
then everybody's separate life and all that
culture built tenements and cathedrals for
the sake of which you I mean I was ready
to embrace every shadow and declare its purport
in a world ever hungry for new meanings
it will pay no more attention to than to the old,
though it loves to have those hot young
interpretations coming, we gaudy josephs
they buy up and ignore. So I opened my druid maw
and chanted a dream of hips and the hips of dream,
the cathedral of gongs and the park of pure money
until I made no more sense than an opera.
Listening to what I had been saying, I thought:
What a lot he had on his mind, how many
interpretations of so few experiences.
He never left his body for a second, never fled
the old phone exchanges of Brooklyn, Taylor
and Esplanade and Nightingale and Nevins,
whose codes still catalogue his coeds and his heart.
He still has his ear pressed to that sweaty receiver
lust-crazed for (he thinks) interstellar static
made by sparrows on the phoneline at his window.

58

DAWN

from a sea sleep I come
and misty elegant ocean liners
alive with adulteries not mine
and small sneak thieves
till bored with dreams I chose

new light over old industries,
the deep red brick of factories,
the mills of Providence and woke.
A yes for cities and quiet highway
out of sight an occasional
car streams towards Cape Cod
or to the city (yes) to the grey
orderly unfolding of our senses

how slowly I come to know the world
and sleep is such a horny place
till this array of phantom integers
this sweet day begins
selfless and full of light and here
once alive one can do anything and
everything is streets and elements and space

even at its busiest time this vista will be calm
and few, calm and few and covered fire
and where are we then, animal
so brisk to start again?
what does it tell us empty river empty street
the stage so beautiful and ripe
before the actors have come and
mouthed their foolish lines and gone?

OIL OF EXCESS

for Patricia Snyder

Our adoration must not be humble—lowness
is no gift to what is beautiful or rules
serene in the hysteria of heroic action
knowing the world her own. Neither humility
nor false relation, as by imputation
an adjective leans upon a noun and claims
at least for an evening to possess it, and in the claim
lies an impertinent definition to which the Queen,
that sum of all our nouns ("Our Queen") might like
to lodge exception. And where is excess then?
Misheard to the brink of the scaffold
submitted to that separation of body from its primary
comparable to expunging all modifiers from the noun.
His head. Her heart. Her throne. His devotion.

THE CITY, TO FICINO

I only know what some thing means when someone
asks me "what does this thing mean?"

(we type with both hands but write with only one—

no surprise then that the cold mosaic of the machine
for all its unyielding sameness of size and size
says so much more the *animal* who
drives the words—those Memories—
before it onto the open plains.

Writing is assembling the animals,
naming them for you.)

*

Then it is raining inside the crystal.
Ficino wakes to hear his Saturdays
calling along the sinew of his arm—

> *Attend my remonstrance,*
> *sleeping man.*

> *What you propose is always serious,*
> *hence dubious.*

With three women you assay the night
going open-hearted to the place
called Boxes where they do the such-and-such
that so excites you—
not a dance at all though they are dancing
in that cafe called The Water of the King.
A fugue from sense inside the senses,
an exposition in prose
of the obscure rimes—runes or rhythms, same—
your blood is always whispering to your brain

fitting this
into that

and being various.
Such
is your *Hilaritas.*
        And Ficino smote
his forehead with his palm,
glad for once at all he had neglected.

    *

A situation
is not clear.
On a mild night he walks in the city,
the three
women are not his mother,
they are actual
as his *nefesh* is, his beast-
breath souled out at
whom he passes
and they do pass

before and right now and to come.
Later they take him in to see
women dancing naked
to delight
that part of the Enterprise
the eyes
hold in sway,
lords of outreach, pure prospect
in the long hegemonies of sense.

Because of these sleazy bistros he is Plato
—non Christianus sed Ciceronianus—
as if every step in North Beach were
a rung up that silvery ladder
leading to transperson'd Formal Love

and yet ever and ever
the same rung, same lust, same step up.

62

Hence men are amazed at philosophy
that they will not be led.

He goes home with one every night
like a man opening a new book.

The love of language leads to language
and where does language lead.

*

Ficino knew that promises
come up like peonies
and ants come walk the sweet heads
involute with neat desires

—a beast is accurate.

But what was his promise worth?
Sense is a contract.
Who can see is obliged to see
and those who look away look
only to self-undoing. He
was not happy with the way they danced,
the blonde automatism of it, fixed smiles,
the little things that let us move—

(who does a smile love?
and where does it lead?)

*

The dance led nowhere in him.
He wanted to touch this one or go into that
but the want was easy as the music is

and like it would stop without remainder
and just be gone. *We watch*
he thought *a pageant of projections.*

Does he mean protections too,
nobody out there not first inside,
no one to damage him with news?

Cease without remainder,
a candle noisy in the rain.

MEASURE

Albrecht Dürer's
Motto: *Halte Maass!*
Keep the Measure!

If the ink is too light for the pen
the rudder breaks off and the boat
tends to drift away, towards the green
horizon, towards a french-speaking port
with ancient wooden wharves beneath its palms.
Priests always lurk around. I want to buy
what you want to sell, we are congruent
hence destinied. There are flags
with yellows and soft blues, everybody
wants the same things—what keeps weight?
what holds measure?—we had to put in
anyhow, for bread and lemons and fresh meat.
I have money, you have time, together will be
a bamboo bungalow on a rainy mountain,
warm rain, fertile terraced hill. If the ink
is too thick pack ice appears, and lonely ptarmigans
settle in the rigging. Whales pass preoccupied.
The rudder works but the world is far away.
At night we dream of a city beyond the ice,
hydroponic parks, cathedrals of pure number,
new friends talking language we can learn.
But the morning is always cold and one more egg.

Albrecht, who *does* hold measure? And when it's held
what manner world consents to be so reckoned
among spasmic pixels of my tired brain?
You came home with sunlight in your head, sun
and the formula for sun. What can we do? Set
word after word until the most appears
and what you've spoken will have been your dream.
So ink must be accurate and full of praise,
apt density, viscous but fluent, bone black
but glistening in the moon your fine ship rides.

And then the gull, that old companion
marked my path by going

parallel to the sea's front
along of a building that had no heart

and all its doors stood open to the wind—
but the gull did not go in.

I stayed outside and understood
an hour, then forgetting what I knew

I slipped inside, surprised to walk
the familiar boards and corridors again

and *Leave me, Leave me* the house was whispering.

AN AUSTERITY

for Amy Goldin, in memoriam

Hot traffic down Route 9
asking commodity
of Saturday, begging Supply
the unfaltering
richness of the world—
this terebinth mind
among the flowering quinces.

UMBELLIFERAE

for Jim Duran,
who told me the place.

Old flower
with thy gaudy
mauve underwear

sit beside the desert and score
my successful amours

so much of me has been push, just push,
till up past Susanville
there is nothing but what there is

we call it wild, wild
or nothing, a hawk,

a hawk over a flower.

When I finally caught
up with him he
with his shoes full of rocks was
halfway up some local
Everest a port of call
for rattlesnakes a bone
baked in the sun

Stay talk to me I never
had a brother
                    "All
these predicaments
I've heard before—
wife and brother, god and satchel,
you need what you need,
you're not so different"

And I, to the shade: Sorry
I can't take your sunshine
—and he:
            "I who was myself Beatrice
and wore the crimson habit of your love
have learned the Exile that you taught me
and go ahead of you up idle mountains
researching an exaltation
                        from which we both
time after time have fallen
into the arrogant cities"

A QUICK ANSWER WEBBED TO ALL HER LIKENESSES

Once a womb was. And
who was Alcyone the mother of,
whose star swings all of us,
strange queen caught in scarlet
recurrences above unseemly text

never yet translated.
How many before you stopped counting?
Space, proudest boat,
you remember every spillway in anticline
the rest the reservoir—
oh they rain each other day in sequins
secret sump beneath overt dwelling
where every 'thing' is banishing.

Laurel scanty leaf'd already in too shade
knows a smattering of transformations
such as Cybele beneath her mural crown
allows to the prestige of demons,
those aliens on the road to Manipur
that city jewel to bask in jungle body
—lianas intrical novemsense astir with Reason—

as I be true to this remember-thee
or sporting speedwell below true aspen
a grommet holds it to the wind
laced with five varicolored scarves
and every time the canvas flaps
it's as an arrow coming home
into the little ox-hide scutch I bear thee
limned with my plain device:
Or, hand having a rose, proper.

2.

Tell the deniers that scorn her silks
they will be various and she be singular
until the plateaux of the moon
comprise mere suburbs of her enterprise
and they can flag or dart or sleep hard pallets
alone with their self remonstrances.

Tell the arbalest makers that the pentagon
unifies the living with the dead
until the arrant pessimist we elected
falls for antic fescennines, then merriment
will bar jejune apocalypses (there is
no fundamental text) and boil the tepid river
and from both banks the phosphor tendrils
leap up from gunsmoke to explore the sky
to find it no airier than your body or his mind
rife as it all is with happening thick
as the pens of a goose-feather or as a cork
wedged between the vintage and the world.

3.

It is a bowsprit antiphon we doomed ones sing,
salt-wet sailing out towards republican utopias
ice stacks havering in lieu of coast
to land among pinguipeds and so reflect
their long neglect, or sample shifted elements
until your cadmium is in the rose again
bowered in idleness
                         (adjust the pronouns here—
for grace is limitless)
                         a rock on a piece of paper
this rock your palanquin Herself
sudden eyed, dare at last to call this flower red,
wake the host of Parthenope from midland swoon
of dark character under cottonwoods
those elegant sturdy buttocks of Nebraska
each gate a speciated name, a nome
of Lowest Egypt where the bronchial sea

coughs leopard-wise in bamboo, severance
from less work than politics.

Darlings I really rede you
and all I taught is how to love me,
avowals of the clericate, every jill
a judaspriest, every interlock a banyan
beneath which only one grows wise—
"soft fluffy floppy Ethiopian steamed bread
then up lank hillsides to a swale
where had been your sunning spot we sat
above it on wet ground the grass
so thick it made a mat beneath us
kept us almost dry" philosopher in clover
heterodoxies unicorn's weak eyes
a spatter of sparrows dusting by
and a hawk over the whole of it!

BEFORE THE REVOLUTION

The notebook moves but the hand
is still. Green trains in Paris
in the subway cuttings
flash. No news is good news still.

Mauve iris on a dish, swamp
iris in a bottle yellow flag.
The long disease that haunts this craft
comes from the wind, and big white birds
(those house cats) make it worse
churring about liberty in the rigging.

For both of us it is a world of rope.

2

A reporter watches bullets pass
and doesnt care. His keen small eye
makes the present infinite.

Our work starts when the body slumps
against the wall, and rough lime
scribbles on the dying shoulderblades

brushmarks we decipher. I read
the coat of a dying man
and study the footnotes in your lap

where by glory I'm permitted to express
the starrier sense this body yields
like waves of crucifixes in a baffled sea.

The chairs come toward us
and the windows have looked in too long.

A house is their delicate polity. They
suffer us but how long.

Even now the carpet is stirring,
the television seethes an Iliad of pure greed
it watches while we sleep.

And the chairs are moving again,
the windows are starved with what they see.

We won them to our cause a while.
Determined, persuaded,
towels writhe in the hamper,
the car meditates a precise revenge
where going turns into staying.

Only the chairs are moving
and the windows would like to go to sleep.

THE MESSENGER

1.

If you dont have much time
a flower will do you

a stack of sweet william
or just dawn light on an old door

You had to travel to see this
and it had to wait till you came

The world is full of such bargains.

2.

Feed the messenger as well
as the kid or the camel
get to eat
        a man
cant walk on sunshine and the moon
leaches iron from his bones.

3.

I got here, what more do you want?
A word
from my mouth could be anybody's.

I'm here, I have nothing to tell.

My shadow crossing your doorsill
is message enough for you.

LAST SONNET FOR TED BERRIGAN 1934–1983

It is about time to say goodbye.
While you were dying I was flying home from India
and we were over Ireland when you died.
Did you ever get there? A flat, stony country
with dithering roads, small, small, I do not
care for that ground. America is the only country.
I mean they almost understand you here
and there are lots of people you can love.
It's a nice place to live, I dont know about dying.
They say it was a hemorrhage in your throat
worn down by talking and holding things back,
because we never say everything we mean.
They'd never stick around to hear all that,
since we have to save something for death to tell us.

ON A PORTRAIT OF JOSEPH PRIESTLEY

1.

Who is this man who signs a face
signifying something known?
What does a face know?
It is an Armageddon that
science comes in, a sequence
of unnatural disasters that
finally leads to mind. Green
mind and red mind and no such thing—
what can I do but reverence your high eyes
pale as a bullet in snow—
frozen morning, a love runs out,
the poet falls. The duel is over.
Not even the lake can understand.

2.

So there are tables that we read
and some we turn, some tap, and some
stand by the window in August light
technically effulgent. There are convents
where pure misunderstanding
sanctifies the air like the lust of candles
translucent on the cold tile floor as fallen wax.
In the abolished library the ghosts of books
shimmer in Egyptian sunlight.
No one remembers. No one comes later.
What is lost has little to do with what is found.
Even their mistakes have perished.

3.

So there are deer that last the winter
in numbers we can calculate.
And the houses of Back Bay take on

a fleshy sunlight late afternoons.
And the river is always a sort of chemical.
Words mean what their meaners do
and what their hearers apprehend—
that is their tragedy.
But there is something deeper than Mu
where words have their own womb
and breed true to type. Disciples with silver
chasubles and brass thuribles pass
through the panoply of molecules
seeking pure matter to pray to if they find.
And still their lips are dry.

.

GRAVEYARD IN NOVEMBER

Afterlichen
where we suppose
a naked one
feminine
draped upon
the cross. After
lichen ceremony
divers green.
Timegreen mostly.

All rock spendshift
reexciting those bones
by due proportion paid
to laidbare
allegiances. This
skin to this blood
returns.

All those we.
Last bastion
of arithmetic
as if the numbers
could also
sleep in god.
I saved nothing
have every
This.

LITTLE OFFICE FOR THE FEAST OF ST JOHN

Prime

This is the day to think about the two of them:
sleeping dancer and dying reveille
the cock killed crowing and the farmer's daughter
barely blooded herself now smeared with his
for her sake decanted and for the mother-power
of which she is the sleek ambassador. War is not far.

Tierce

A sentence like a dance goes on
until the listener, that bad king, can bear
no more and craves the naked end of it,
the meaning itself shivering in torchlight.

Sext

Ordered pair: a Salome, a John.
A saint is an extremity of passion
or dispassion. These are such —
a truth more important than life
a lust more important than truth.
It is an honor to think about them,
dancer and danced, the hip and the head.

Nones

To say she danced with her feet
is vulgar; he talked with his hands
too, like any one who doubts
that language alone can bear the word.

80

Vespers

Her dance was body and his head was heart
in a world where only flesh can bear the word
it takes the two of them to speak
and all the rest of us to silence with our greedy listening.

Compline

Dreamlessly repeating dance and death she sleeps
and wakes next morning puzzled by the dry blood on her lips.

FENNEL

Looking for something to stand some long trailing soft leaves of fennel in, I found my tallest glass. It had been a candle, the kind that Caribbean people use on their votive shrines, and we had used in some similar way, other senses of deity, other realities, the same flame. I filled it with cold water, and arranged the fennel in it, the leaves, the thin, less edible ends of stalks, then set it up high on the refrigerator, in sun. Then I saw that the glass was imprinted with a prayer to San Miguel, el arcangelo mio — My archangel, do for me what I cannot do for myself. What is that?

In a stalk of fennel, Prometheus stole fire from the god realms and brought it, anxious, well-meaning proud demi-god, down to the human design, most persistent of his gifts. In a different tradition, after humans, unaided except by good counsel from a slenderer, sinuous anti-god with glittery scales, stole some hint of knowledge, self-knowledge, an archangel was appointed to stand, with a fiery sword, at the gates of the paradise their presumptuous science had entitled them to lose. Fennel and fruit of the tree, angel and angel, titan and serpent, the same flame.

And I thought how fennel, left in just such a glass, gradually loses the vivid green its ferny leaves show now, turns yellow, though not flame-yellow, and smells bad, and makes the water it's in smell worse. A smell I encountered for the first time not long after a visit to the morgue to identify the putrefied body of a friend I loved.

Prometheus tells us, through Aeschylus, that his most energetic and deceptive gift was a concealment, a taking away from humans of the realization of the certainty of their deaths. Stripped of that organic wit that knows how to die, men tumultuously breed and scheme, as if and as if. Always they begin by tearing down whatever they find around them from before — they call it fashion or progress or modernity, but we know it is the gift of Prometheus, working like a hormone in them, to deny the obvious inference of death from the works of those who came before us. No more myths, we say, or no more history. Now, we say, live now, taste this. The fennel sits in cool water, already by now just the temperature of the room. As it turns, loses color, it reminds us of the nature of that flame that bans us from immortality. Mortals who doubt their mortality find no fire in the fennel stalk, only a sweet, fresh taste, like licorice.

What do you do if
as you walk along a street
ordinary under maples you
suddenly smell inside a house

not just the kitchen
but the hallway and the sittingroom
where Uncle Joe has his feet
up on the horsehair hassock
and the *Times-Union* slides
from his knee to the floor
and the carpet on the stairs
needs vacuuming? What do you do
if the house is everywhere,

and you smell the bedrooms too
even the one with the door closed
where Lisa and her boyfriend
claim to be watching tv,
or the one with the neatly made bed
no one has used since Christmas
when Aunt Vi passed out on it?
And you don't know any of these people
and you've never been here before?

All this romance
is just Zanzibar.

What matters is a note
stuck by a magnetic carrot
to the refrigerator saying
Dont look for me I am gone.

THEORY OF PLACE

It is always enough to live, isnt it,
the theory of place, and the sign of waking
every morning in the self-same bed
as if it were a part of your body now,
this soft pale thing. Your mother had one.

Men desire your body vividly
but when you wake up in it yourself
you just remember Grandmother
dying in that very bed. A soft thing with legs.

2.

My love is such a curse, isnt it,
such a nest of interlocked reminders
that reproach you for not doing everything
you ever thought for a minute you
wanted to. So powerful is thought.
As a swan is said to drink milk only
from a bowl where water and milk are mixed,

or as a lover can sit in the room
and see nothing but the curve of your neck
where it kisses into your shoulder
and not even notice the blue anemones
you carried home in all that snow.

TOO MUCH ABOUT THE DANCE

The old serenader
sweats under straw boater.
Blackface makeup
streaked now, the pink
of Protestantism
shows through; his collar
stained, regrettable, is Irish.

They cavort and he sweats.
Their limbs, perpetually
cool in flowing clothes
however fast they flash.
Their arms fling,
he bangs his strings
remembering Whorf's essay on [fl-] [fl-] [fl-].
He sweats. Frequentative.
Repetitive. Her dance.

And his song:

> Sit down and let
> your garden grow.
> Be sumptuous a while.
> There is an evening
> in your softness
> I would share, dont be
> so anxious there.
> A body never has to prove
> a thing, or have to move.
> A goal is when, what,
> you stop looking for.

But all that wise music
is wise in his mandolin,
cant get it out.
Cant shut up either.
Itch and twitch, sad vaudeville,
they cant hear the words
anyway he doesnt even say.
Sex is the same thing, but in the dark.

Every poem should have twelve things in it:
(time, measure) season
a flower or something like money,
women and men, an arrow
flying towards a target, some sound,
a part of my body, a part of yours.

SAGITTARIUS

To shoot is not always to kill.
There is an archer's moon
you let fly at with your only bolt
and always and always you find
the arrow back in your quiver again.
To shoot the moon,
go all the way, and the moon's
still there, fuller if anything,
teasing you to be regular
so it can change. Change
and keep coming again.

There is a midnight archer
who draws your bow for you
across the ceremonious resiny gut
of Telemann's viols, too sluggish
for Bach's fiddle, draws
and never lets you go.
You think:
I am a bow drawn across a string
for eighty years, and never do I rightly
apprehend if this is music or
a Scythian hand is aiming me at the dark.
Or in the dark. Toward a letting go
that may be silence only or a flight,
a hissing shaft slicing nowhere fast.

EGON SCHIELE'S BRIDGE

Any image is a boast of mind—
not some thing. Believe the vacant.
We read the wrong books, speak
dead dialects. What difference
is the color of an eye?
Whether some hair
grows straight or curls
loose over a pale shoulder?

Even in spring the grass is gray.
I will not ride that pack of horses
over the lawn time. This is the body
and no word or blood can make it mine.
Some girls are coming towards me
naked, in tight red shoes.
Love is no midnight, no benison
that stammers from the sky
one me, one me.
Love is a southern wound.

THE TOURNAMENT FROM WHICH I WOKE

The wild chirp of the alarm came in the thick of the battadure
After the heralds had shrilled out the vaunts of their cities
And the jousters were pricking their horses host against host
Over a tourney-ground strewn with the white robes of noble virgins
On a field high above the whole city, the spire of the Duomo
Rose over the shoulders of men after a woman in
White slashed with lavender satin had conducted
The magnates and their wives to watchpoints in safety
And I doted like lust on the neighing of stallions.

THE MONUMENT

Though he had made a scant
hundred women happy
a marble statue was undeserved,
turbulent uneasy crotch
swelling under the fig leaf,
his whole posture arguing
haste to be gone.
                        Yet he stood.
We do not know what makes us happy.
What is stone of him is here,
when all the tedious arguing
and turbulent waiting stop one morning
and we are in a state of being happy
suddenly, uneasy because undeserved.
This scant repose his sudden monument.
And then once again we are waiting
where waiting is the opposite of staying
just as much as of being gone. Waiting
is nowhere, the crotch and the fig leaf
carved from the same stone. Without morning
the scant day is suddenly here.

"The flavor of being wrong came to me usually
a minute too late but now on time. At the window,
being sure neither of shadow nor the other thing
that rears behind the cloud a reminder, like a church,

of that luminous engorgement from which we were born,
every one of us was, when the fitful traveler
alit at last in the luminous hotel." When you use
(usually) a word twice you mean, dont you, its opposite?

"That it was dark in there? And dark out here
guessing at motives, knowing it is wrong to interpret
any relationship as simple as good-bye? Yes,
yes." You mean even that, each moment, there is a womb

from which something less certain than a feeling is born,
but still is born. A grove of equivocations not
without path. "You get the gist of what I mean,
or what I meant, but not the taste of it. It's gone now,

the lawn is ordinary, isn't it. I was wrong,
without repentance, and the small causality of it
closes its formless hell around me. There is more of me
than succumbs to it!" I saw it once too, at midday,

a park near the Pacific, someone moving along the lawn
between me and a huge blue eucalyptus. "Formally
familiar, unpersoned. And did you dare to speak?"
She did. I heard, but did not catch the name.

DAMPIER'S VOYAGES

In buying horses pay no heed to the haunch
but the eyes only, the slight
enlargement of the spirit that means speed,
or mild abatement of the wit
that speaks docility. And if a man
seek both qualities in one mount
he will not find it in this country.

So counselled I took ship
and found the contradiction
everywhere I looked,
but there were islands I have not visited
where energy and peacefulness
may look from the same eyes
like a green table in a wild garden
beside a wooden chair
the color time painted it,

and on it one sitting
crosslegged at the knee in repose
reading this book of travels
more with the mind than with the eyes
and those same eyes
lift from time to time
away from table and book
to the rim of the garden wall
barely to be seen beneath wisteria,
looking at the sun through shadows

and the legs recross another way
and the islands in the book
teem with wild swine crashing through
plantain and bananas, their hoofs
under wild spice trees
up to the hock in years and years of fallen cloves.

I wish it was me and not the north wind
made those nipples rise
on a spring day in a white tee shirt
heading into it she
passes my ambushed eyes

themselves surprised
she's dressed so lightly for
spring is no more than a name now and
lust no more than a name and you
and me together make

just one more unpronounceable word.

THE MAN WHO LOVED WHITE CHOCOLATE

There is an egg in the middle of things
a blue racer a kind of whip
to top the spin with, thus reify
(thingle) it, there is a mallet
tunking metal there is a frog
lucid gel that harbors comingstance
the drift of spawn along along,
there is a gong goes in the egg
wakes him from his appetites.

Be scant, new citizen.
Intellectual hedonism of easy things
well-made plays, craft
for the comfort of some buyer—
yet no shoe without its nail
—sails look cuter with no boats—
so many ways to get married

and live in affluence as you'd live in Spain
silently well-servanted on gaunt plateaux
surveying our meaty ruin: O vultures
(but they respond not, being robins,
sparrows, such, and common crows)
having their own jive no need of his

there is a white taste in his mouth
long row of stalwart fencing
dangled in his neighbor's light
unstrung from rollers and stretched
along the bordermind, a tooth
for you, muchacha, and (lachaim!)
a prick or two—galvanized roses—
in your hand. Willingly obey the dog.
Go. (He reflecteth darkness as
rehearsal for that sweet despair
that long Without)   blue flowers

red birds new grass a yellow chair
a flag of surrender run up
in the smooth colorless air. Eat me
said the day, I have never snowed,
never forgotten. Bird thuggee,
rattle-pinioned raptors throng
devour such offerings, raw
conversations between parted lovers
estrange him from himself. Some stars.
Admit that appetite is mostly mind
you're left only a little tool to lie with
—the cardinal almost orange in harsh sun
swelling towards the river where she sits
red vestmented chatting with a friend
who cut her hair too short—
who pulls me down? See, see
where an old chunk of weathery wood
checks, splits, gapes to show
Christ's lordly tulku in the firmament.
Even this, heart, is one more thing.

The talk is chaff from off some core,
coronal of disasters whose livid petals
one by one we dare to pluck. Blue flower
never found unless in losing.
Many a burnt hand, mortgaged mind,
undersapped foundation, leprous wall.
Leviticate, lixiviate, then levigate
—one more lie from the makers of the Pantheon—
in the harlot's church a dead emperor waits.
Le tombeau de your last concrete example.
Broad skated, high on the wave, prorsum, prow.

Hone your keel for such thick seas.
A moment after. How is she now,
and will her new car mend the distance?
Spill a road on whom go quiet
gyved by circumstance, not wearing a hat,
wind-tousled, a shy conquistador?
Malinche, remember she. So dark.
Weinend, klagend, Easter never,

hope not, live long, squill-blue, hurry.
The spring is in today, no wonder
like this wonder. A lamb in trouble.

Fondle you. What world does she generate
sexier than herself, and if none, bother,
she-failure, one more just plucked rose.
O she doesnt make things up,
the villainess, does she suppose
flesh's enough for flesh and talk for talk,
aye-bartering, yatter and sex?
Tisnt. Rub two random words together
to get a richer universe than any this.

Micron by turkey feather turning
we doubt our same black bodies and white bodies
because the difference is only a car only
on roads capable to go that we have made
and there's no finding He didnt find before
—the man who ate rice pudding
without necessarily liking and certainly
not despising it—one turns
and it is here—lactoglycodynamo
a kilocalorie or so to wake
what part of us can sleep—
red baubles on a spruce tree, April tinsel—
o the horn signal of the house on fire
whence even skeptics flee—here comes
the hook and ladders!—spirit searchlights
spotting a hasty ruin—hurry—
promise the little children something red.

Promise levanters a sensuous occident
and they'll come home, every sentence
is the whole of what he ever knows,
but he has no home to take them in,
that's rich, that's lips. In palaver
linger, between a breath and a breath
glimpsing true orient—as when the words
you suddenly see her mouth making
are only to make you look at her speaking

—at and in—beyond and never come home
—that were promised-lander's promise,
pure going! Pierce going, pang getting,
all at once a devious love-feast (a door
for him suddenly open) listen (opera
that curious machine ('feel my heart
beating where your ear hurries')
lords and ladies coltsfoot the periwinkle
blues (husband of a breast) (cantilever)

the man who loved white chocolate
loved a rumor of the sea
that one of those milky camerlengas would
(hard to see through tressures, hers, as
today she of the sky said, *treasures of cloud*)
float him to a book or book to him
sage under carageen an old unlogic
unlocking—the greatest mystery is analysis—
to demystify the very sense he sees them by,
utter,most,wise,ness, the continent.
Not by any mirror see your naked face.

White-stubbled cheeks a youngish mien
six finches at the window bumming seed
gloriosos full of chatter and
strumpet-minded he sees gold
beyond the greenwork of the day, spring,
lax, oil, tight in posture loose inside

I am the uncommitted
grotto of Natural Selection
what he thought when he went home
thinks him forever after or not ever
—the bust of Beethoven on the shelf
must mean something—take it
in small mouthfuls, mind—

look at the season you find a self in
so well calypso'd you'd
guess there is none, you'd be right,
stomachers on cold bacon, a chest

full of medals he cast for himself
gorgeously enamelled — Arkansas tart
her fanny smelling of patchouli —
George Sand's fingers trail along the keys
in private agonies of emulation —
I wear this hero's cross beset with jade
for the Campaign of the Hypothalamus,
this ruby wheel, this ivory of spinnaker
for all my frowardness, mirror jabber,
testament of thieves.

It's morning and he's full of sperm again.

THE DOGWOOD THE ANSWER

The dogwood is no answer
it is opulent wax
the moon finally in our hands
and this is what the moon
smells like in our atmosphere
this night of ours
that needs so many flowers

2.

the gypsies I remember were dirty
too clever to be dangerous
too languid to dance beneath
the moon really belonged to them
who else could own
so costly a thing, sellable,
undeliverable, the dreams
of unwed mothers

3.

the houses that we had had iron
gates or hedges so thick
you couldnt see a girl through
though she wore a bright red jacket
and her iceskates jangled in her hand
and you could see her breath above the knotted branches

4.

it is what comes down the street that makes us

5.

the street the street the ice
alarming autumn catches yellow
elm leaves in, Batchelder
south to Avenue U, in those days
not very far from the sea.

MY CITY

The cathedral has never been finished
and one wall of the museum
is permanently in flames.
What can you do when you can't?

When you can't trust even art,
can't trust the seals
in the seal pool to stay seals.
Can't trust the marks on panthers.
Can't trust the signs.

And that beautiful woman ahead of you
bent low to drink from the fountain,
how do you know she won't have a cat's
face when she looks up, or no face, her hands
the claws of an osprey slimy with fishgut?

Nothing is known for sure. Not even poverty
is safe from chance. Cobblestones
melt in the vapid late afternoon warmth,
pigeons crash into the sky and fall.

LIKENESS

a theory of Mashal, for
Morton Enslin, in memoriam

There is no home
in resemblance
(as cat piss the June ailanthus),
who can live in likeness,

fragments of one self, studying
the lore that is god (going), the dark
that is god (coming), the god
that is no one, every, who made
nothing, nothing made,
                    the Monogene
of the Moment, last born
of the whole world,
measured and reflected and held?

Go now before the cat comes back
or the owl tries to sing. Go
while light is in the leaf.

FOR THE ASKING

Things that are always answering
take a dim view of sunshine,
that answerless question.

A woman neither plain nor beautiful—
what is to be said about such an one
with the wind in her blouse and her hair
provincial, fragrant, abundant, wheat?

And the lamb in the lee of its mother
on fat grass under a rainy day a little cold
—an individual, or only some case-ending
of an inconceivably distant noun?

And what about adverbs, infinitely, sadly,
durably, quickly and with passion
instinctively finding a friend? A seven
year old girl finds a robin's nest

and how about the four turquoise eggs in it,
how will the mother bird know she touched them,
if she touched them (how could she not touch them,
how could things ever leave us alone)?

All these problems have the same smell,
petals of a meager spray, white lilac
belatedly I break off in the dark and bring
to the attention of someone I love

saying Here, from my angry island, love,
these delicate
and precise only because you'll see them so
flowers are invented for you.

OF THE SENTENCE THAT SPEAKS ITSELF MORNING ONTO BLANK PAPER UNCONTRIVED, AS IF SUMMONED BY THE BLANKNESS ONLY.

And from what silence waiting steadily
do these first words pour? A muscle moves,
a lid that blinks at metaphor, refusing
likeness. If there is sense it lies in difference.

Do I accept the same a language makes?
("He'd better.") Grovelling in the lubricity
of homophony, like that knight
(who will not fit the meter) who sported

his soul away among oily Thuringian hips
of imagined women, but whose yard
flowered, last triumph of uncontrived
resemblancing. A flower to the mind

as a girl to his dry stick. Or do I read
wrong again the measure? Heed better
the point of passion between immoderate
pleasures—grammar of bodies

musics dances wines willingly—to give
everything into this moment so that all
you are slips utterly into the world of it
like a word from the mouth of someone

startled from sleep—thinking neither
of waking nor meaning nor thinking.
And here the antic similar is again,
neither fact nor fancy. A convection

pattern for philosophers. A broken harp.

The Pope told Tannhäuser: You have worn out your imagination creating and peopling the Mountain of Venus; your brain is burnt up with fancy. And the knight crept away five hundred miles, grieving, despising the Pope but having no doubt of the diagnosis. Then in a cold country, his body worn, Tannhäuser's pilgrim-staff broke into leaf, then flower, so that all could see. The dead mind worked again: he cried out a woman's name and in his mind's eye saw her coming to him, she with all her sisters. And they took him into the condition he had imagined.

FOR MY FATHER, ON HIS EIGHTY-FOURTH
BIRTHDAY

Father, I suspect that I've done all the things
you ever wanted to, wanted with the vague
intensity of your pale eyes, and left for me.
Everything but sing at the Met—
but if I had, it would have been basso, not the clear
Fra poco a me ricovero you wanted to lift
bell-simple, without vibrato, to reach
the dingiest altitudes of the Family Circle
where you stood in your day to hear McCormack's
soft little voice swell to fill the huge hall
impartially.

        In a season of tiger lilies you were born,
when Victoria still had a year to live
and the river, our river, was not much different.
You have looked out the window all your life
and what you saw created me. The faraway
of your eyes! That cats have, and holy men,
samadhi with a cigar, but never a word
of what you know, *there,* in the unbeginning
unmanifest permanent that leaves
a certain light in your eyes while you talk
of young Dwight Gooden, our latest hero,
striking out eleven surly Cincinnati Reds.

Quiet and the shell
opens
a sound out
beneath any sea
we may have happened
to hear —
          something
far, itself, no land
in sight, not
all this island music.

TOWARDS THE DAY OF LIBERATION

(for George Quasha)

It doesnt matter what we see there

(the mouth is full of sense
no taste in listening
no sense to hear
what twists in the shallow water below the tongue)

(and if he says Listen! say
Drink the hearing with
your own ears, a word
is not to hear)

Language? To use language for the sake of communication is like using
a forest of ancient trees to make paper towels and cardboard boxes from
all those years the wind and crows danced in the up of its slow.

A word is not to hear
and not to say—
what is a word?

The Catechism begins:

Who made you?
Language made me.
Why did It make you?
It made me to confuse the branch with the wind.
Why that?
To hide the root.
Where is the root?
It lies beneath the tongue.
Speak it.
It lies beneath the speech.
Is it a word?
A word is the shadow of a body passing.
Whose body is that?
The shadow's own.

110

MEDITATOR

He settles down on the lake and becomes a swan.
Decoy. The more he swans
the more they'll come.
From over the tamarack at water's edge
flying low, as if from inside the land
itself from which he came they come.
They settle round him, a throng of wings,
until their truth (they fly)
pours into his deceit.

"PRESSED FLOWERS OF LIBREVILLE"

for Harvey Bialy

I heard,
with a street on the edge of town
unpaved, my feet and their feet
after a little rain
just the same color, we are built
by weather, you were there,
you should know, there is no
place that does not make us its own

and this line of yours
is not your flower and not mine

nothing is ours but the saying so
we think when we are very young
(Rimbaud, Peter Rabbit, when ducks
are white and lions reason with their prey)

and now we know nothing is ours.
Nothing. It is like your father
bent over you some summer morning
smiling, saying Get up

we are going away.

What is attained has no idea.
It is him. What is left
beside the road is the side of the road.

In the small
hours when your body
is answering me
I listen
to the bare voice
no more wanting
to press in,

the furrow is full now
of fallen wheat
spent rain
star-blood the penetrations,
asters, there never
was more to me than desire

listen, never more than
common fire, I lied
I told you stars
I am only and I am only
and I am old, my hair
is the color of your hands.

I am in a ring of beggars,
little baby beggars in their beggar mothers' arms,
eyes vague with disease, their chubby hands
reach to my face, child beggars already skilled,
bold because it's still half a game to them,
jabbing their open palms at me, slices of emptiness, eyes
bright with teasing, prowess, scorn. Strong adult
cringing whining beggars who have learned
fear, imperative, shoving their begging pails at me,
old beggars silent and crippled, on all fours,
all threes, stumbling erect, whining on the edge
of the beggar-mass, fixing me with the intense
vagueness of their eyes, only lovers
have such vague eyes. Blood-painted and rotting
beggars, the leper at the edge, his eyes gone,
face gone, only a gaping mouth-nose hole
but his claw comes out to me too, special silence
of the leper, all the beggars converge on me
and all their eyes are mine, all their frightened
greed is my greed. And I do not look at them.
Above their heads, beyond their clamor
are all the shops around the square, each
interesting, full of signs and merchandise
and colors. There are temples and odd
trees, mooching dogs and hill ponies at rest.
This is what I came to see. All these
I look at, lilac, pistachio, the curious fading
of mountain colors, rock-red, sunflower yellow,
grey white of so many clothes, the sun
in a blue sky.

The beggars whine, I look above their greedy faces and my
own greedy eyes devour store fronts and architecture and bodies passing
and all the different colors of the world. We are locked in one greed, these
beggars and I, no difference. At the moment I am an intersection of greeds,
I feel the clamor, a big pressure in me to break out of the circle of their
greed and give myself over to my own. What I want. What I need. The
alms of difference. What I came here for. What I want. What I want.

You break a mirror
and the face is still there.
Where?

A time gone?
Idaean Paris come to choose,

come in shoes,
white-spatted Belmondo as
if Paradise were 1926,

you could still buy Gauguin
water colors, Amy,
Belle, Cynthia, Diane?

Their colors were truer than trees,
skies, the little train
to Fontainebleau, Elise
liked to be slapped in autumn,

under the elm trees, yellow silent
except to the hand,

forests and memories, how
archaic. How little.
I needed chrome,
distilled of time
I needed sleek recencies
to show my poem to advantage,

my lekythos, my tapestry,
my gilded head.

Little time in all its currency
jangled when I walked,
all its tenses and subjunctives
conditioning my face, blush,
lip varnish, a hope
for her or his
favor who was quick,

unbold, savory, hungry
like me for the sheen of things

and like me confident
that the way to possess surfaces
was to penetrate.
Not depths, Idaean
wastrel, not Hekate, no, the jab
in and come out again,
quick the letting go
that lets the skin the smooth
recover its surface blossom,
tension, poise,

a light the Louvre never knew.
Then I was born.

THIS ANIMAL HAS BEEN SET FREE

it says on a cage in the zoo
but beyond the bars the same brown eyes
stare sadly past me
where zookeepers prowl up and down bearing incense and candles.

SONG: FOR THOSE WHO COME AFTER

Learn the new way
whatever it is at all
the beginning and what will you do
the end and what is done

learn the green mistakes
your father fell
and when you young
are beautifully wrong

when they teach you
loving say No
say Yes in the middle of No
be kind in emptiness

no one knows anything
so believe them all
a style is seduction
and worth a kiss

but dont get married
learn ships and wind
and all ways to go
when the tongue leaves the mouth

and the sky is not just money
and the sea is mostly wet
and Anywhere Anywhere
your lovesong your anthem

and Everywhere Everywhere
should be your mother
ask nothing but to give
and never remember

what you'll never forget
a bright road running
when you want nothing
and there is no different from here.

AMONG THE SAGES

Sometimes towards the end of a year the calendar
sets fire to the wall, the cellar
joins the sea and over the small trees
cones of light upwardly unfold
that make this small place a galaxy outward
to its near neighbor stars
while down in here the cat attends
the inside of its left hind thigh
and crows discuss the unusually warm November.
Nothing shows when everything is changed.
Flags hang limp in the damp inhabited air.
Nothing is lost and nothing is found:
this balance lights the universe.

THE VALUATION

If this were a painting and not a poem
I could sell it for $3700
and spend a week or two in the Antilles
watching black people do those
graceful menacing things that turn
so readily into art. Then back
to my 100-acre farm in Delaware County
with moss on the pigsty roof
and a thermoplast skylight over the kitchen
makes my latest blonde look washed out
with winter light, her hair
with smudgy roots. But as it is
it is one more unavailing poem
tinged with economics and envy still
trying to celebrate in a way Pindar
might have respected the deep
sacred green of the soft persuasion
of moss on the roots of this little
wet tree in Rhinebeck on a January
afternoon, everything ordinary and eternal,
pallor of named things, this little tree
without even a father, this poem
with no price and no meaning, only
the veiled destinations of the heart,
for you, the goal of time, reader,
forgetter, relenter, cherisher, no,
it doesn't quite work, does it, the poem,
you can't forget you'd rather
be smiling at a significant picture
something insinuatingly beige and crimson
on the firm white plaster of a wall
you actually own—hint of permanence,
not just sonorous allusions. The moss
is at the center of this, it's getting cold,
tomorrow morning this soft nub will glint
with ice crystals in it, poor moss,

poor words we forget so easy. Yet
this is what I want to do, this dying
image is what I want to give you.

A myth may not be everlasting
but it wakes up before you do.
There is Perseus in a steel mill
with eyes on the bodies of women
rescuing them from the rocks of employment,
unemployment. Flying them
in his arms to the garden of madness.
Absolute silence just past the edge of the city.

KABBALAH NUDE BY NATURE

The great air accepts even music into its hands
        another life
        a goat chews a quiet leaf
and here the trees are noisy cold nights creaking
store your light in the cellar where Need is
        I am back
to the mother avenues and father tide
        the bleak of childhood
with no book to decode
        what should I be thinking now
and no story but my untellable own

for I was not this place
        (I am this place)
or any street the bus roars through
        (I am this street)
peach pit from August asphalt
        shot suddenly by bus
tire passing back to wooden porch
        chipped the paint by my foot
(when will my love come)
        I am this street
        dusty ruby
adventure coming for me a girl
        a father's car to Rockaway
        eating clams
in the smell of sea much low tide bounty
        (was I the moon
the chemistry set, the crucifix? the door?)
        I was the door
through it to this now there is
nothing but mathematics
the girl came in the house I had
        nothing to say
but the smile and the kissed cheek
        on the way

now there is no room to take in
and only I esurient, craving salt,
          sugar high, wood beads,
peach gum, craving but not wanting, full
          and hence silent
after the overfurnished dinner of his life
          trumpetable
insolences a door open, a light on
          did you
and if I did it was mine to do
          broken letter
is that window sparkling yet?
          we need it in winter
two or three times a day
no other exercise no other air
          body language
how the sky falls away from the dance
Sappho in the spine, all my friends' daughters
          wake this appetite
does anyone imagine me to exist
          caltrop
falling always dangerously pointing up
          across the hall a woman whistling
uncharacteristic the whole world stilled around her
          into the world.

REVERE BEACH

for John Wieners

There is never
too much to remember
after all our neurotic tries,
a liberty is in the cards
somehow connected vaguely
with taking off clothes.
Nakedness never works,
the beach never cures the city,
summer never heals the year.
But raise my daughters
with red hair, anyway,
architrave of a temple in Futurity
where we go to learn what weaves,
What works. Over-
   specified desire, festin d'amour.

Come quickly back I may be going,
and who will orpheus you then,
mild one, among the remembered?
Old address books harry and confuse me,
her name excites me, I feel a happy lap,
I cant remember who it specifies.
A name and a feeling, no face.
And she with all of it may come back.

Who knows when they'll work their way
here again, full of August and watching comets
and nibbling chicken livers in Brookline
wearing shapely grey knit dresses
and being named Paula and listening to
Brandenburg concerti on KLH's, it all
could come back again, every autumn
is fronded with young women
reluctantly but firmly making
claims of exclusivity on me.

O the years, the years and never let up,
watch the elevator doors slide
shut and remember the smell of their shampoo.

Quiet dementia of a winter night
the stars pole-axed by a burnished moon
and everybody in a trance.
A lot of white in everybody's eyes.

VOCATION

Months worth of notations
from my researches in Real Time
with my mouth open.
Poetry. A neutral term, equalling
something made. Made out of love
and lust and dictionaries,
crinkum-crankum and thin air.
The sum of everything.

I mean the hum. That old
Hellenic mistake, archaic.
Who? Sue. Sibilance,
histamines, hurry. Poems
have as their effect in chief
a conspissation of the lower air
into a more lasting whimsy
recurrent among men. Listen,

I dont want to sit and type,
but float garmented in light
in the middle of the sky
retinues of glorious silences.
And there by speaking let
them kiss me with wet noisy lips.

JANUARY

He hated the feel of the watch on his wrist,
liked the cloth on his knees, early
as it was the sun strangely low.
Ah winter, we never believe you enough,
cruelest of all the mountebanks of time
with your daft promises of resurrection,
it will all get better, crocuses come
like the eyes of 19th Century philanthropists
turning steel profits into Gothic comfort stations
for mind and body, bless them, self-made men
never forget they have ankles and bladders.
What had he forgotten in all the comfy dither of waking?
Selfishness is always awaiting
personal saviors and private salvations.
Houses are the strangest philosophy,
twenty thousand homeless seek shelter in New York.
The gentrification of the heart has to be unreminded
of those nasty unbelievers the poor, undeserving
envious and coarse, his mothers. In dream
he had forgiven a blonde woman. She smiled then
and swayed at him hips like the sun
leaning into the clouds. Noon, and would never be normal.
There is no medicine for the joy that ails him.

APPLES OF SODOM

for Melville in Judaea, lonely

If in all thy nonce deceiving
Man thou bitest on a gem-rind fruit
whose pulp be yet sourer than thine

are not then Equals met
when each discourseth to the other
on all the tricky gauds of kind?

NUEVA YORK

> The Trylon over Flushing Meadows — an upside-down
> exclamation point, the sun its dot

This city
is something the sky said
and said in Spanish.
Being clear only about edges,
sneak up on art and remember.
Not art. The marriages
proposed. How many entanglements
slipped I, and how many wives
sneaked from my palazzo
back into the public fact of mind
refusing me? A white lie
pointedly kind, so often told
I came to credit it. One more
deft escape, out of the window
of their lives.   O women
I took you
with only the moon for your dowry
how can I wonder that you come and go
and while you're here are very beautiful
before the night comes when you dwindle
in the pale dusk over Hell Gate
until even the river runs away from you.

THE POET

I never believed I had something to say
but believed in what I said.

—This sincerity, was it good for you?

For years and years I've gone on cutting
from the best leather and with skilful cobbling
shoes that fit nobody's feet.

YESTERBITE

That domed reprisal,
National Park of Hell
(memorial
to what has never loved
another never
been a self
freed into the exquisite
transgressions of nowhere)

has been liberated by the Interim Army of the Morning
again, and this time
Col. Kelly's communiqué
has a firmer tone, We
are dug in and we are
changing, everything
you remember into
the grand geology
(he likes the phrase)
of just what there is.

"By midafternoon the common soldiers
will lounge around the Cryptothèque
all lost in the sense of found
where the last treasure is
(enfolded in the linen of music, many violins
not playing loudly, but the vertical
array of their differences, sounding)
on the shingle beach, Bristol Channel,
prison and sorrow, sepulture,
the archeology of light
we call astronomy,
Orion over the river
this last of all our tonights.

And again I have something to say.
Men move like monkeys

and I am tired of all these weddings,
the unred unrocks of this never desert.
Bruckner's 5th.
Every music is past.

Past the drum called me
inside my head
this is not yours
not not any more
it never was, just
the sunlight on Metambesen
and Baron Delafield's untrimmed woods,

a business in land."

I couldnt tell
if the burr or buzz
was from his throat or mine,
I bow to him
who unlocked the difference

cudgeling my head
(drum) to breathe
an air remembered
inside a well-cut new grey wool coat
so pale in dawnlight
reads as blue:
I am trying to breathe blue

without the international contraption
of Orpheus loudly for his wife complaining,
distracted by every whimful girlful vector
that passes him from zone to zone
along the battered road of the indifferent
seeking a tomb with some sun in it,
the great mild-venomed snake of the equator
lifting to watch his music.
Dance.
A head is rolling by.
It is the drum of difference

lost in the nineteenth
century city of my insides,

Manchester City Hall and Les Halles,
a fine unmarried banana wrapped in green waxy
paper florists use
to amplify the landscape of the bunch
they part with for money,

"and what do they buy?"
and who can buy a flower?

White zinnias before the altar,
a quondam rose or two
and one still ardent
color of the inside of the heart —

anfractuosities of seeing
things and remembering
not them but where they stood,

vacant rooms in sunlight,
parquet corridor polished
towards the muddy street

as if by envy we were civilized
and love's absurd flute
were always summoning

lost women to come home
between my good right
ear and my left ear

deafened by the hurry with which I heard.

THE CLOUDHERD'S SONG

Never having done anything ever but watch
and never having actually watched anything,

never having attended to anything but cloud
and never having touched one or learned

its numbers or colors or rightful names
(except once on the slopes above Darjeeling

I woke out into the morning and breathed you in,
mother of atmosphere, green air,

eternity, vagrant, the monsoon
had brought you and I took you entirely in)

I call you cloud and call myself yours.

Cambridge

A WOMAN WITH FLAXEN HAIR IN NORFOLK HEARD

in memory of Basil Bunting

Wherever you are,
in any season,
I will come to you
from the flowers

she says, and always
call me
by your native language
lest men
think I am strange

or a woman known
only in books,
I am steady as sky
and no further away,

see me in your own
color, my lips
shape the same myths
you live inside,

whenever you do this
I am with you,
to kiss you often to sleep
or wake you
sudden or gentle,
a mouth
in the middle of things.

2.

In dream I learned
a book appeared
in 1732 using
for the first time

in English
the word *'ud,* glossed
'oriental religious
meditation'
                I know it
as a lute, the very
word is womb of it,
a music
to grasp firmly
in the left hand
and sing with the right,
sing with the right,

this *'ud* means
strength to hold mind.

3.

Planning to move into the country
one thinks of how suddenly

nothing is nearby. A city
is an hour away — the condition

in which it is common to breathe.
A city is the same as air,

never-ending effort, unifying us.
And you are a young

married woman whose parents
are buying a house in Trunch.

It is funny to say the name aloud,
and funny to say a house, or an

house as your husband, the joiner, says.
As if you and we and all

lived blonde or dark, doomed
in a fresco on a wall

in one of those churches people like us
drive all afternoon to visit.

We are saints of a sort, gaudy
in our private way. We mean

something, but only the churchmen to come
will be clear about what we meant

moving and removing and walking the dog
and falling silent at the breakfast table

and checking the sun and looking away.

Being sure about where things are
is not the same as having them between your thighs
like a horselover's horse or a wife's man.

And there is a spire on Salisbury
and a gilded flèche on Notre Dame
assailing the impassivity of heaven,

the immense infamy of what does not talk to us.

And if the moon is as you say
funny-looking and fragmentary
in a sky no cleaner than it should be
(something stuck to something else)

and if just looking up and sighing
the way we do, we moon-watchers
(humans), measurers, neighborhood
historians, amorists, weather-poets,
cloud-herds, weapons dulled with
oxidation (phantasms of night),

gawping (in other words) at the moon
does no good at all, then we seem
and seem to be stuck with the ground
(the shelf we watch the moonlight from)

and everything that goes on down here.
Uh oh, the neighborhood again.
Mrs Grimaldi. The bus. That stupid dog.
The girl across the street with bad
complexion on her cheeks but how
I dream of her all night, my mind
stuck on her like a moon on a sky.

ANYTHING NATURALLY ITS OPPOSITE

Tell *me* a rose a change!
Were you even listening?
Is it a capillary that brings
it-is to *it-will-be*?
One asks, one walks
back across the Square du Temple
with a quarter-kilo baguette under arm,
shares a crumb of it with ducks and pigeons
under the cemented rock crag like a zoo's bear pit
and pulls one's jacket close against the cold;
flakes of pewter chipped from the sky
fall, a cat sleeps on its head beneath the hedge.

Naturally opposite.
Nothing is near, nothing
interprets me.
We woke around a thing my
body found itself doing in the night,
a prong right up out of dream
you found and amplified
until it served us both
passing in and out of the barrier,
membraneless border of
tight-juiced ecstasis — *there*
in the place for you which is most *here*.

The ways words work
or don't, sudden stop
of meaning, a door
but a lock on it.
I used to love hacksaws and peachpits,
the rough irregulars,
biting through the steel shank
and the lock suddenly jumps open —
a life opens from this.
A curve decides. Let a curve

decide. Let the sun
come out and confuse you again,
such weather. Blue
makes the black blacker, white
whiter. One bar of Cadbury's
eaten slow down Fleet Street
and into Covent Garden, walking
in the names, but the chocolate
is another order of the real,
thick in the mouth, experience,
hard to swallow, sweet.

Then what is here? Is it another,
a clematis to be planted by the porch?
It's 82° today, as if winter had not been.
And just yesterday. The electric
blanket's still on from last night.
And over the foggy streets of Ghoom
lament for Govinda, is it,
I hear from where I am not?

Hearing by absence
love of the truth.
Tea in Camelot, a ruined
purple wrapper, a chunk
of the chocolate itself
dropped down among ornamental yew
outside a restaurant as offering to
an earth we can pick up and wield,
Buddhalocana, an earth we see with.

Are you listening?
If no more than eight hours it is running,
sound of feet within this watch,
a falling.
Is it sand falling past the eye of God,
Sandman, Gower Street, put
my love beside me on the top of the bus
in the very front seat where all
the city unrolls from us, from us
the avenue uncoils, we

who snake the whole eternity
with local destinations
from Victoria to Camden Town
o let this love!
A city neighborhood is a section of God.

2.

Play in the garden,
Mother of all Living,
heartfelt, arabica,
azalea, a symphony of Gorecki
to stun the silence with.
Woman's voices.

First of the seven bowls at morning
water for all the beings in the world
(how big is that? how wet is water or
where does it end,
deathless tangency, horizon
itself dissolved, solution?)

and then a bowl for the Teachers' feet.
Pour this into this, citizen
shaping the earth. The good.
Museum Street. Coptic Street. The clock
ticks in sunlight, isnt that weird, what
does light have to do with
the mistakes we make about time, that
for example we can measure
Great Russell Street against a
dome of soft light lifted
just before dawn into the parleying of gulls,
white-workers, few
cats we saw —

Where is the King now?
Asleep under her wing.
Where is the money?
Stuffed in the hollow oak

where all our names are embedded in springtime.
Who is younger than I am?

Norfolk blended into Holland but
sharp edge to Kesteven, the lights—
"nothing that way, pure open sea till the North Pole."
The retirements. The age.
Good Friday and she goes west again.
A new word needed now,
we have heard this word before.

Just a word re-echoed under the old bell
telling the hours? Telling them what?
That York's walls run in sunshine
and the river is neither answer nor question.
Sit down with me here and be my book.
Handle everything you ever knew.

Whose face running which way
was better than this the other to?
Or do? Do you know?
And if you don't, why
are you listening to me?

Is it all about interruptions,
about grass? Wheat sprouts,
and rye does, and any ritual you eat
can engage the light, the word
you wake up speaking from the belly
at first waking when her hand
strays near you. Me.
I try to write *me* I write *men.*

How long since he would see him again
a confusion of times like the whorled
imbrication of petals in a rose

all history is like this, nothing is clear,
neither why the elm trees are all gone
nor why all the others followed off North Broadway
in Red Hook or anywhere else, breasts in a blouse,

148

eyes shaded from the light, a sweet girl's voice
full of money, well, it's about time,
it's all about time, we have no other tissue,

the heat alone of the hand makes a mark on glass
to match each fingertip—tripping
in the back seat—having fun all alone now,
saxifrage, aster, skullcap, dittany
I kept the empty humor of our naming
—battle in the cathedral, the miracle,
water flowing upward and to the right,
stone stairway to the chapterhouse at Wells.

3.

Flat sun on an early April day—
O there's the American who thinks
to hold our interest with his weather!
No wester snow this week than Gloucestershire.
Flitch of need rotting in the flesher's window,
Lockerbie. A girl for me
imported from the oldest language.

(A woman carrying leaves
from one side of the visual field to the other
coming and being come. Low wind.
Who is watching, or saying. Or who is worrying now?)

They're not fog lights, they're the eyes
of a small Jersey town looking for justice—
"all they gave us was money.
We believed that paper gospel and we fell."
No equity in money, no survivance, no sheep
shape moorland whose springy turf
argues a having beyond all ownership—

This sullen energy, the one warm room in England,
what I permit myself to art, smell of *hing*,
old name, title of the energetic what or where
but only one (breast in a handcup, tongue
rimming someone else's lips, say, a landscape,

or from Paul's dome the gilded shopgirl who weighs justice out
stands far below over the Old Bailey,
blinded against the forgiveness of the impartial street.
For who can sin against the sun, or break
the light's law? No real law can be broken.

O the crimes of art even before committees,
the blurring envy where self-love
denies any other workman
and all the gilded Nazareths of his wit!
When artists forgive each other, the world begins.
The house goes to the country, the wall
glows from the image, the jocose maiden
slips off her skirt, her white
nylon smallclothes from Japan, whose boat
floats in whose Serpentine? Whose reign?
Whose miracle? Having just stopped wiggling
Elizabeth (painted by James Tissot)
stands suddenly poised in a doorway.
You can hear her ready to laugh. What
is behind her? What is outside?
The outdoors. What handle has been
carved for this whip? Dressed in white,
ready for the Fair. Whack whose beast
a street away, stuffed from a rainy breakfast
or in gaslight. In yellow. Under glass.

But what is news? So many choices
and not much choice. The door
is near the room, the room is near the floor.

Light is near the window, heat
lives by the candle. She takes in
what she can, or a little bit more.
The rain of prophecy
wets her thighs. The evening is divine.
In all this misery there is a quiet exultation.
The heart of being good
as Friday is. This, or all year when
African armies land in Labrador
and move south, suppressing looting to set

150

up an ordered polity again.
This still is Egypt, my dark place in you,
lap of a gypsy girl, a simple melody for trumpet
rising in thirds.

Good Friday 1985

A LANGUAGE

If you know your mother's brother
and your father's sister's husband
and they know your name

            1) a cat with a snake in its mouth
            2) sun on the garden
            3) sun in the garden
            4) a wind that meets you on the roads

someone is dead.
Whether you remember it or not.

"I am hot there help me cool"
running across the plane sector

            5) do you like it with milk in it?
            6) will you come tomorrow?

[Lesson 2]
of it
if
if a man [mi] goes ['gro] [na], then.

If then. If then, then. If then, then then.
Patterns (repeat) if. If if.
To look at people and be fascinated. By them
though they're not doing.
Is it fascinating to be fascinated? It is if.
If not, not. If what. If it is. What is.
If what is. If that. Repeat.
If a man goes it, does it bleed.

In the garden stands a tree.
                      Notice the substitution.
                      As.
In the rice paddy stands an umbrella.

152

Count the changes. What is its nature.
Nothing stays the same.
mi-rtag mi-brten

In the garden does it bleed?
If a man stands an umbrella in.
If not, what?
Is it fascinating to be it, to a tree?

Applely.

If not to be fascinated what stays the same
must be a substitute.

Otherwise nothing stays blue.

*

> The sun on this beautiful
> so hard to hold opaque
> instrument against the light
> o all those sayable things
> I am always saying
> but Montague Street in rain!
> is different, and the spire of Amiens
>
> If I could learn this river

*

(A language is another language)

do you) ever remember me walking in your sleep?

Any smile sunrises the fleece. He woke
and saw the little hill littly (lightly?) covered with snow.

gangs-seng   *ri chung-ngu gcig*
a snow lion   a little hill
                                                            from an early age
language refers to what you do with it

(What is the English word for river?)

Bracket. A river. Never.
Opaque lake.
                    Such touches
                    I gave you madame,
    I ask you to return them now,
as in a cambric folded
                         a dozen and a half grey
                    linen letters
whose brown ink obsessively almost repeats your name.

And all the rest of it I say I say. Give it
back in me again, let this breath I meant you
mean nowhere now.
                         Reach your majority, hurry.
Let me be you where you take off your clothes.
(Plagal Mode)

                    I   see   ,   you   .

The same space left for meaning as for,

                    what I mean.

                                        [End of Lesson 2]

Lesson Three is black Exercise One begin
to enumerate. One, one, one, etc.,
One, etc. Is it really
or is it yet?
Strawberries on your white plate.

Almost summer now. A cotton
for you. Somewhat river.
Grandmother has gone back to West Bengal.

How urgent can we forget?

                    5) a street of strumpets
                    6) Depressing the clutch, relax the handbrake.

154

(One word.) Do it again.
7) Notice the sparrows making free with the
grass seed. (Two words, not *grassseed—

"Three esses in a row
In one word shall never go."

8) elegant pain
9) Could they contrive a way to cool off Laura?

With respect to this, that is big.
Comparison
always needs one leg
tethered to the tent peg, so we know.
This lesson is about what we know.
Say anything you like in your new language!

Exercise Two, a stapler, an incense burner, a fox. Etc.

10) The quiet gate opens again.

Do you remember (above) how to use the Key?
If a man goes it, will she burn?

A letter, how. Dear Sir or Madam
    I have never been sure—   [*nges don*]
(the moment of your mother's name)   [*ming*]

Dear Surly Adam I have
never been pure but always
pure is somehow in me
let it
let it and love me
best of what I would be am
if I amn't me)

an amnion. A purity.

Views of the cathedral [at Rouen?]

space supported
by our glance alone.

And how about the change? A language
                    spoken from the Channel
east to Lorraine. A name   *ming*

precisely doubting. Hear them, my King!
                    Believe what? The same.
Always the same, from the island in the mist
                    supinely coming, came.

It is where you *are* from, the truth
                    or the Northern sky.
The rest of me is south, no chance or after.

This anger in me, can you break an ocean?
                    Can you hurt the sky?

For it rages simply against what is all round,
                    the bad music of other people.

He said, and the century changed. Canals
mucked over with pond scum. The railways
churned and ran and stopped. The sky was gone.

ELEGY

Alone alone is not a touch or need
to dwell with sheep archaic pastures
who was a rock small in sunshine builded
at last upon some pediment — prominent
carved with one more god's name.
Lust is terrible desert. The burnt lizard
and the parched lioness alone are able
to construe that name. Now the phone
sings and a thousand signatures
finally answer my mail. Cubist
conversations watch women pass
talking to one. So much skill
to be a martyr or fake an erection
because nothing is simply simple. *I will go*
because he borrowed my attention
but want to stay because I love your milk.
Transparent to show the works inside
fairy with dew or with the morn's pretenses,
streets, those false premises, leading
deeper into an unfathomable argument

I still have to pay taxes to.
City is all those women I do not know
to say the least or buses where I will not go,
bars choke on what I do not drink.
Still sitting on my lap so lift my hand
beneath your sweater that our eyes
bask in cognitive relations
before one more dawn comes back.
We are not a population,
we are one at a time ones,
not individuals but handily distinct.
"Mysterious, like everybody else."
Avid ascenders, satined in glory.
Our hearts are just like yours
you tell me — but not a city,

which is the sum alone of all our ignorance.
If it came down to it
would you have to sleep with me
to know what I mean or let me go?

Or would the last revision
leave a text as desolate
as the evening star just
before the full moon rises
in blue March—nothing
but words and what *they* mean?
Only a story storying no one,
chastely, ceremonious?
I want to come between you
and your lips, your graceful
concessions to this language
we drown in for our oxygen.

(Sleeping far away from one I love
is not so far, is not alone
the way alone is. It is a word
spoken and heard, the pause
before some answer comes.)
A slipper full of cream
to walk on stars with—
what a queendom you intuit
and frame it with your thighs
—pale borderers—play
chess for breakfast and
breathe all night long soft
wine of counterpanes and be
lush as any Apaloosa is for
meadows, any steel for
cantilevered bridges over
estuaries mobbed with birds,
pelicans, loons, shearwaters,
a man is an animal who looks
and lives in cities, steals
glory from the trembling dictionary—
while lust is a pigeon safe
on any roof, head of any

steeple open the church
and where are the here
in your hands I also come.

Gets me nowhere. It is sleeting outside
and wit is thronged with tasteless things,
combinations and resemblances, a feast
of cheap interpretations, a sleek
modern rhetoric in the slipslop rain.
Always hanging out in other languages,
or is it snow. Drove home slow
down the mountain and by the river
imaging certain blond adventures
I would not consent to if I could—
the heart has a chastity the mind might envy.
Give me a diamond to give it to you.
Make it hold water and break light
with blue promises. Flash after flash!
Desires are savages surrounding you,
respectful but determined,
chaste as knives,
these things that go on knowing me.
Fantasies protect you
from taking the real as real—
because they move, and that motion
is real although the mover's not
and he courses in an unearth landscape
chasing hot phantoms. But such
bright ghosts they are, with such soft hair.

Movement moves. Absolute predication
without an absolute to predicate.
Real worlds
have no rules,
just consequences.
No taste
without its mouth.

(if you talk long enough to the robin on the lawn
till your heartbeats and his hops are in sync
when he—ruddier at the breast, no bigger—finds

his worm, what do you find? A chill
of huntingness, a morning with no soap,
a sense that you are nobody, hence clean and true,
true as hot and cold, or things that come and go.)

The one you heard on the radio reading out loud
was a cloud. The wet slick on the porch roof later
was his idea. There's no harm in calling him a god
if you reflect that gods too have their limitations.
Cant have bacon for breakfast, for instance, or fast
like your girlfriend on green clay and psyllium seeds.
Or do anything about the world's misery they too
will ultimately share, even in Wagner, even
when their silk brocades smell funny and their pals
remember prior engagements and even the peaches
on the trees of heaven fall bitter pulpy on dead lawns.
Pray for the poor god who gives us comfort while he can,
wind and rain, a wise remark or two the thunder passes.

Examine the tracks of animals. Passing by night,
reading by the neat light of stars which way to turn
when there is no real way out. See how to run.
Under a pine tree the tracks gave out, a flurry
in the snow, then nothing. Where did it go,
such a big animal, a wounded deer, lost
by hunters who suffered their own distractions
and were not as intelligent as it was
to begin with? Where does an animal finally go?

The form released from killing and from craving.
The form released from fear. One daffodil
and then another, another, and she loves me.
To seasons we are like any beast obedient.
Indeterminate links to what determines us,
a boundary demarcation some fool pope proposed
—as between Spain and Portugal dividing
a thing called body from a world called soul.
And we are various, five heaps of praises, five
heaps of undetermined gypsy othering we call our own.
So many bodies it takes to be me, and what it is
is hardly anyone. There is no folly

160

like the myth of philosophy. From no landing strip
no airplane takes off for nowhere.

Jungle edges of an infinite population,
field effects of gossip. Local history.
Time was the man who. This was the idle boy
who grew to be the man who never rested.
I look back to long days of those summers
when I did nothing but dream and eat and read,
rose into reveried air, look back as
in the afterlife mind might look back
with chance compassionate nostalgia even fondly on
the soft awkward body that gave it so much trouble.

There is always a lonely house in the mind
where it is sad and black birds only
come to bring the news. Sometimes red
patches on their wings remind us Springtime
is still available She is really there The glass
fills up and empties The sky
is always empty. That is its gift to us,
its art, this emptiness,

to have a working knowledge of the world.
Little alabaster carved to seem a bird
with a whistle in its tail. South American.
It's hard to blow, soft breathy siffling.
The bird itself seems to have turned round
to see what our mad lips are doing now.
A bird like the Egyptian letter 'a,
glottal stop, orange beak, lazy eye,
posited on a rock of one substance
with itself, looking back, complete.
You can barely hear it in the next room
except you know that something odd is
happening. Someone is calling you.

A SAYING I GREW UP HEARING

"You could eat off the floor" they used to say
about women (usually German) who kept neat houses
(clear plastic tarp over crocheted tablecloth)
(where are such women now?) and on the piano
sheet music from Saxony, marches and ballads,
nothing too far from our deepest lust:
to be at home amongst familiar things,
to be stupid and doze and leave the kind sunlight
for flies to explore. At least we live longer than they do.
It is strange—the sun lasts longer than the earth
yet each day we survive its dying. Light.
What does it mean to sleep and come again?
What does it mean, to be comfortable?
Where are such houses now, with etched
looking glasses, with biersteins, with ashtrays
no cigar ever deflowered, with large mauve
and indigo flowers woven vaguely in beige carpets,
with milky coffee, with one piece of cake?

DIRECTIONS FOR A LIFE FULL OF BLISS

When it moves,
watch the movement.

When it stands still
watch the stillness.

But when it moves
watch the stillness

and when it stands still
watch how it moves.

SHAKESPEARE

Fear no more the and how
did he in mild England know
how much the day's heat was to be feared?
Sweltering Tenth Street nights, or Kansas,
or Bengal—where his language runs to hide
in straw and palm shade—where a day
climbs from the cool morning high
into the blazing, sweat is the ocean
that drowns these eyes, *fear no*, how did he
take the measure of our far weather?
Was it the language told him,
putting this with that until the truth appeared,
spoke its mind and fell
back into turbulent silence?
No man ever listened so well.

FAREWELL LETTER

There are not many ways
to tell you this. The cat
jumped over the moon,
I married the spoon.

The machine of difference
has ground us apart. You
are blue and I am west.
Only the brass & silver bell

in the middle of the sky
keeps us together
by hearing it. Already
I cant tell it from the rain.

A RIDDLE FOR ROBERT GRAVES AT NINETY

The rock they are carved in
Lasts longer than rock.
Everything that happens
Makes there its mark.

Longer than rock and quieter than air,
Almost permanent they are
Hence easy to forget. Every lust
And every dread are part of them.

But they kiss nothing and fear none,
Stars in the daytime are more common,
Letters birds leave with their feet in dust
Are easier to read, though these

Belong to everyone, are at home
In every language. Constellations
without stars, currents
Without water. Tracks

In the snow with no snow.
Nothing matters and everything is known.
The unhewn dolmen weds
Perfectly the hole prepared.

That there will be kings again
that parliaments will fold
back into towns and shires, that the red
legs of geese will strut
over London lawns, that brass

will glow green and copper blue
and freemasons meet in drafty
lodges under ground, that men
will be devious and fierce,
priests fell, children wanderous,

and women bear no contentment
to be ruled. Again the tree
will be our Pantheon and rock
some lichen grows on will be our Louvre,
and words like 'we' and 'ours' will leave

a sarcastic taste in private mouths.
The world comes back again and rapes those
who thought to make a meaning
we could not share with ants and sparrows,
a lovely thing, a chemistry,

a thing indoors.

Nothing is finding. Red hair is not red.
The squirrel sitting up so cute
Is not thinking anything you think.

A park dissolves. If weather,
Then behind a door. If Africa, despair.
Something is everywhere thinks

The assassinated leader as he falls.
Pigeon shadows flutter on his dead eyes.
One statement follows another

Forever, meaninglessly different.

A WEEK AS WORK

This bone is my brother. This soft red
this pulp this meat my sister. How you
become is someone else. Taste me
and know my difference, I am the sudden
world. Swallow me and change.

Monday

When I am a coin it is tomorrow,
work reels its workers in on roads
and it is bad. Thirty these make one that.

It starts out every morning painted white and then.
Whatever others want happens me.
Take me I am ample in; out of me
is out of luck; no fear remembers you men.

Tuesday

The day after anything is a war.
Byred in arrogant simplicity, the old
shirts of rich people starched with sufferings
not theirs. And they do too,
secretly, in vast houses, among uniforms,
shielded from bodies, at night,
hardly listening, vomit Limoges tureens
full of turtle soup.

That world be done.
Rip that girl's skirt off
and run it up the pole.
This world is after anger,
after hours, drunken sailor, salute thee
commonwealth of our capillaries, blush,
hurry, only one in the sky five billion below.

Wednesday

Numb, we wake. And then
suddenly yellow, an idea. In the middle of a thing
like a cow in a barn, a snake leanly licking milk,
a sparrow nobody sees. Every image is a politics.

You cant think about anything that isnt
something you're thinking about.
Then blow the wind, hark. Then
analyze the market, who.
Then babble on the bourse, do.
Then half of bread and half encyclopaedia,
for that thy merchandizing's never mute,
nor dumb the vowel of thy credit instrument.
What is dead, when? is only always us.

Thursday

Dead middle of what is past, a power
if only to go on. "Mocking our hopes
turning our seed-wheat-kernel   [Sylvester's Du Bartas]
to burne-graine thistle." This
that is not the world, is the world.
It's worse than grain that doesnt sprout—
it thrives indeed, and drives our virtue out.
Malignant musics, oafish parliaments,
addled physic, bedlam surgeons, the croak
of power from its blank basilicas,
o dome me lift, by the middle of the wick
there's hardly any light left. Scarce
any me or thee to benefit or heal.

Friday

This little life we love in
something close or by all accounts
different as cheeses. It is to touch.
He-geminis doubting their election to
what was not grace. No collar like a dollar.
One size fits all. And no one—great

170

Grimpen Mire, flight on footback, moor sedge,
wild cocks calling hard at the edge of dawn,
the East just a smoulder before a black fact.
He gave a moan. Even this day
to the pit shaft, the soggy traces where his boots
or ears resounding from the automatic hammers
a thousand feet down, children of itself the rock.
Who could hate better than they have to hear?

In this place your death will find you
never more than twenty leagues from the sea.

Saturday

The rush of money up your tract and down
is quiet. It is another and you something sleep.
A feather to your credit. Brave weather
like an enemy, sunrise not different from a bull
crazy shouts over the horizon. Sometimes is so Paris,
Gare du Nord on rain sky set, say, or he forget. Slips
again. Forgeries, oxhides, terra cotta
stamps cooked in a Carthaginian fire—
nake her now, wake! he does, and the curtain sags with light.

Here it's. Both shut. A feeble in the armor box,
seeking a good opinion of himself he slept for two.
It doesnt work. He's free today and nothing looks,
his arm soft sleeps over his headache
and on the tip of waking he forgets her face.

Sunday

So nothing was ashamed of you but the sun
would not live in that awful stone box. Your mood
exalted easy sparrow thought, but there, in silver,
in drunken Father Brady's hands, the Cup made sense
from which the senses staggered into this muscle, mind.

That gleam of grey morning was the eye of god and god's
eye in its gaunt grey theology was just
such a gleam of something more. *What is God*

the shadow of? they think, and shuffle
up the aisle to tell by tongue
all afternoon while Monday waits to swallow.

LIFE SIGNS

He jumped back from the mirror
embarrassed in his quarterback's jersey,
his hand still messy from the acne
he had been studying with his nails,
a young man disturbed
by an older one, me.
While I stood at the urinal he fled,
leaving the mirror for me to read my wrinkles in.

Orpheus. As in orphan. Alone
not knowing how he came into the world,
into the gift. Orphan: writing
without occasion, without intention,
without situation. Song
from pure desire sung,
pulled from the lyre, lyric,
the music of the actual,
tune of what is merely the case.
The best of him. Having
neither parent nor child
he sang a sound or word
that hung in the air
a while, in the empty world a while,
as if it were listening to itself.
And he heard.

2.

That is what it means to be Orpheus,
to lose her, always, and always in love,
into the same dream that brought you together.
To lose the foundation of your life
so that even the rocks and trees are free
to move, around, dance, and she, is free
of your hands on her heartstrings.
She must break your harp.
Who are you in the morning, then,
after the snake of Eros has bitten her
and escorted her off into the dark —
where precisely you cannot follow,
you who are in love with only her.
Down there they are in love with everyone.

174

Into the phantom city she goes
musicked by love, enchanted by the love-swarm
that streets around her, love love love.
And still as she goes, around her feet
in shadow small quail are calling.

TURQUOISE

There is always another language to learn. Massive silver encrusted with turquoise and jasper, or is it coral? Where would they get coral in Arizona? The fat man is studded with it, his wife too, saftig but not fat, except her breasts bulging out over her bodice like clusters of jadeite or jasper, massy globs of semi-precious flesh, a little time on them. My teeth ache to bite them. This is language, where it comes from, where it leads. Things that have color: coral or jasper, dull soapy red.

turquoise, sky-green.
coal, black as money.

While we are only 130 miles from the sea, this elegant fat cowboy with hair luxuriating down his back to his 54 inch waist, stubby under his stetson, crudded with gems y plata, he seems more to the point than Captain Nemo or your latest masterpiece of the whale business. Where you see turquoise and jasper, it means: Nothing changes here except the clouds. They're few enough to count, or read, or translate with our dreamland snores, our dying breath.

The waitress wears a sky-blue dress. It is the only color I remember. I look at her, up at her, up as I once looked up the brick wall of our house and saw the wall falling down on me, and leapt back; then I learned that it was the clouds, moving, moving up there. That the sky moves. Everything is two years old, the famous Italian Renaissance, though tired, is still going on. We are still learning perspective. On the bottom of my check she has written in blue crayon, Thank You! Kim

She is thin, the cowboy fat, his lady in between, where most of us live now, right around the corner from the British Museum. No matter whether it's the one in Brooklyn or the one in Bloomsbury, on Montague Street it's always raining.

Suppose when I stood in the furnace room, my hand on the throttle the door knob was, and listened to *Tuxedo Junction,* or, more truly, when I heard it come on the radio and ran to take up my post at the door to guide the whole house along the tracks of the garden I could see coming through the twin panes of the furnace room door, all of me and all of it moving in such perfect synchrony, an observer in deep space would detect no motion at all, for all the speed of house and child and music, no motion at all except the busy self-effacing spin of the planet Earth, also in perfect rhythm with our movement.

We do live in between for a reason. That's where the meat is in the sandwich (beef on wick in south Buffalo), where the ground is we dare walk on (not the abyss, not the sky), where the juice-sponsoring wellhead is to which we hurry from either side, to penetrate with rude or suaver prong, or else be born. We live between, a grand columnar thigh on either side. We live in between, poised on the endless Equinox of conscious life, the permanent simultaneous orgasm of Suchness and Awareness (Emptiness and Wit, Kindness and Bliss) we do in fact inhabit or infest.

As you can tell, I am, looking for the sea. It is my supposition that a transform or desinence set up in language will lead us there. Where we very badly need to be. Everything is changeful but only the sea knows it. The creatures that infest the sea are occupants of change. The sea has no weather but change itself.

If men weren't so physical women
so emotional a relation
ship would be as trim as any if

and if women were not so physical men
so emotional the ship they mean
would slip between

wave or sidewalk crack
and sink down to the true
center of the all-there-seems

—seas sorts stars tribes trees—
till travel
ships them soft together forward fast

skin oiled skin
slip if by if and them to be
one cauldron of tolerated insecurity.

POEM FOR MY FIFTIETH BIRTHDAY

How many birthdays
I know myself through—
the girl in white slacks thrown
into the swimming pool, Narrows-
burgh NY 1949, I still watch
the pink soak suddenly through—

under apparency, the skin,
the actual fact! Listen
to the skin, you luscious
overweight music scampering
to hide the fissure of your ass,
the dark trine of your liberal bush
in the rumpling giggles of white towels.

Then study it there, the girl
gone, her squelched footsteps
drying on the umber tiles,
poolside, people happy, happy
to have been handled, to have seen
and been seen, straight through
to the absolute skin.

                    The fugue of sense
never lets one theme go.
How many years do I have to see
her hip-happy embarrassment,
hear her happy shallow protest?
It was another time. It stays me
there, where none is passive and
none acts. A middle place,
teal blue like the water in the pool
from which the red of lust and the clear
yellow of intelligent inquiry both
have fled. With her. Into the cabana
from which demure she will saunter

presently in a satiny beige dress.
For them it's over. The strings
engage me still. Second theme:
aftershock of something seen.
I can forget nothing of what I never knew.
Only my actual life deserts me.

TO THE READER (2)

I am concerned to examine in practice how through the composition of poems the organs of enlightenment begin to open, begin to work for the benefit of all. For the benefit of all, not just the talker, the poem shapes itself in syllables, breath patterns, deep metabolic rhythms it borrows from the writer — signal of what is personal (body) transcending itself into what is sharing, shared:

Speech, the deep sound of language, the blood of society, the archaic system of phonemes always focused currently, precisely, urgent semantics of everyday 'meanings' and all the magical guesswork of the mother tongue

that reveal the mind. Not just or especially the mind of the individual writer. The poet is someone with nothing to say. What is revealed in the poem is the mind of all beings who use language, locally this language, this American. The mind of life speaks us in detail for and to which language is responsible.

In the condensing text the poem works all the ordinary and extraordinary knowledge that comes its way from our searches among libraries, annals, archives, dreams, meditation, ritual, introspection, conversation, argument, analysis, lovemaking, daydreaming, looking, remembering.

Then the musical powers of syntax, all our listening, line structure, sound, begin to act: the poem. A poem is activity, a nest of deeds which reader and writer share, transpersonal, unpossessed.

And what they share is one focused, coherent dance of all that's going on. The activity of poetry is to reconnect the reader and the reader's society with the underlying ever-present glory we take as behavior.

There is an internal politics of the poem: that the spontaneously arising text is responsible to all the constituencies the poet contains and represents, and is contained by. My obscurations are my wisdoms. My needs are my permissions. What I hear is sacred: in one ear and out the mouth.

The poet's prime responsibility is to esteem nothing unworthy of notice, nothing too small or too large, too subtle or too obvious, to talk about.

To learn how to say everything and to keep silent.

Silence is the life of poetry. Not the silence of the uncommitted, but Vimalakirti's silence that shook the world, the silence that hears us at the end of every line of poetry.

Photograph by: Suzanne Iseminger

Robert Kelly was born in New York City in 1935. He lives in upstate New York, where he directs the writing program at the Avery Graduate School of the Arts, and teaches at Bard College. He is currently working on a second collection of short fictions, *Doctor of Silence.*

Printed April 1987 in Santa Barbara &
Ann Arbor for the Black Sparrow Press by
Graham Mackintosh & Edwards Brothers Inc.
Design by Barbara Martin. This edition is
published in paper wrappers; there are 250
cloth trade copies; 150 hardcover copies are
numbered & signed by the author; & 26
numbered copies have been handbound in
boards by Earle Gray, each bearing an
individual poem from the series *Objects
in Space,* inscribed by the author.

3 5/88
3- 5/88
3- 4/08